101 ESL Activities:

For Kids (6-13)

Jackie Bolen &

Jennifer Booker Smith

www.eslspeaking.org

Copyright © 2024 by Jackie Bolen

All rights reserved. No part of this publication may be reproduced, distributed, or transmitted in any form or by any means, including photocopying, recording or other electronic or mechanical means without the prior written permission of the publisher, except in the case of brief quotations in critical reviews and certain other noncommercial uses permitted by copyright law. For permission requests, write to the publisher/author: Jackie Bolen: jb.business.online@gmail.com.

Table of Contents

About the Author: Jackie Bolen...........6
4-Skills: Higher-level...........7
   Draw an Idiom...........7
   Human Logic Puzzle...........7
   Interesting Story and Questions...........10
   Picture Prompt...........11
   Quick Read...........12
   Reported Speech...........13
4-Skills: Lower-level...........14
   Ball Toss...........14
   Categories...........16
   Dialogue Substitution...........17
   Dictogloss...........18
   -er Dictionary Activity...........20
   Is that Sentence Correct?...........22
   Q&A...........23
   Role-Plays...........24
   Running Dictation...........27
   Sentence Substitution Ladder...........29
   Word Association...........30
Speaking & Listening: Higher-level...........31
   120-90-60 Fluency Activity...........31
   20 Questions...........33
   Celebrity Talk Show...........35
   Five-Minute Debate...........36
   If I Had a Million Dollars...........37
   Just a Minute...........39
   Me, Too!...........40
   Round Robin Story...........41
   Story Picture Cards Sequencing...........43
   Talking Bag...........44
Speaking & Listening: Lower-level...........45
   Basketball Vocabulary Challenge...........45
   Board Games...........47
   Bumbling Blindfold...........48
   Chain Spelling...........49
   Charades with Speaking...........50
   Deserted Island...........52
   Draw a Picture, but Someone Else is Talking...........53
   English Central...........54
   "Find Someone Who _____" Bingo...........55
   Flashcard Sentences...........57
   Hidden Object Pictures...........58
   Hot Potato...........60

I'm an Alien..62
I'm Going on a Picnic...63
In Front of/Behind/Between..64
Last Person Standing...65
Memory Circle Game...66
Memory Tray..67
Musical Flashcards...69
Mystery Box...71
Password..73
Puzzle Finder..74
QR Code Hunt..75
Show and Tell...76
S-O-S Game...78
Steal the Eraser...79
Student Engineers..81
Talk Show..82
Telephone..84
Typhoon...86
Used Card Salesman..88
Vocabulary Apples to Apples..89
"What Can I do with a _____?"...93
Where Are They Now?..93
Would You Rather...94
You're an Artist!...95
Reading...97
Concentration...97
Correction Relay..98
Disappearing Words...99
Extensive Reading Context Clues..100
Flyswatter...102
Find the Reference...103
Stack Attack...104
Story Timeline..106
Vocabulary Word Hunt..107
Word-Definition Match...107
Writing..109
Chapter Response...109
Character Problems and Solutions...110
Choose Your Own Adventure Group Writing...111
Make a Sentence..113
Name 5 Things...114
Proofreading/Editing..115
Puzzles...116
Q & A...117
Scaffolded Writing Prompts..118
Scoot...120
Scrabble...121

- Synonym/Antonym Brainstorm Race 123
- Vocabulary Square 124
- Word of the Day 125
- Word Poem / Name Poem 126
- Icebreaker/Warm-Up 128
  - 2 Truths and a Lie 128
  - Alphabet Game 129
  - Boggle 130
  - My World 132
  - Odd One Out 133
  - Part of Speech Review 133
  - Punctuation/Capitalization 134
  - Review Race 136
  - Sentence Word Order 137
  - Subject-Predicate Practice 138
  - Word Choice 139
  - Words in Words 140
- Before You Go 142

About the Author: Jackie Bolen

I taught English in South Korea for a decade to every level and type of student, including every age from kindergarten kids to adults. These days, I'm living in Vancouver and teaching English to a variety of students. In my spare time, you can usually find me outside surfing, biking, hiking or on the hunt for the most delicious kimchi I can find.

In case you were wondering what my academic qualifications are, I hold a Master of Arts in Psychology. During my time in Korea, I completed both the Cambridge CELTA and DELTA certification programs. With the combination of years teaching ESL/EFL learners of all ages and levels, and the more formal teaching qualifications I've obtained, I have a solid foundation on which to offer teaching advice. I truly hope that you find this book useful and would love it if you sent me an email with any questions or feedback that you might have—I'll always take the time to personally respond (jb.business.online@gmail.com).

Jackie Bolen around the Internet

ESL Speaking (www.eslspeaking.org)

YouTube (https://www.youtube.com/c/jackiebolen)

Instagram (www.instagram.com/jackie.bolen)

Pinterest (www.pinterest.com/eslspeaking)

4-Skills: Higher-level

Draw an Idiom

Skills: Listening/Speaking/Reading

Time: 5-10 minutes

Age: 10+

Materials: None

Optional Materials: Whiteboard

Give students an idiom and have them draw a picture of it. Then, have them share their drawings and elicit possible meanings. Finish by giving them the actual meaning and several example sentences to write in their notebooks.

Procedure:

1. Give students an idiom and 3 minutes to draw a representative picture.
2. When time is up, have students share their pictures and elicit guesses about what the idiom may mean before telling students the actual meaning.
3. Finish the activity by giving students several example sentences or scenarios using the idiom for them to write in their notebooks.

Human Logic Puzzle

Skills: Listening/Speaking/Writing

Time: 5-10 minutes

Age: 7-11

Materials: Flashcards, answer grids

You probably remember logic puzzles from when you were a kid. It begins with a short story followed by clues and a grid for keeping track of the information. In this activity, there are clues but no short story.

In advance, prepare a grid with the terms you want to review. The terms should be listed across the top while blanks for student names should be along the side. With lower-level students, you may want to use this for jobs, animals, actions or other terms the students will be able to provide clues for fairly easily. With higher-level students, you can use a broader variety of vocabulary and they can give synonyms, antonyms and/or definitions.

Before you begin, you need to select student helpers/clue providers to go to the front of the class. Give each two flashcards, and tell them not to show anyone. Give the rest of the students the answer grid and tell them to write the student helpers' names.

In turn, student helpers/clue providers should give one clue about one of their flashcards. For something like jobs, they can describe where the person works, what they do, etc. For animals or actions, they can act it out and/or make noises. Let the students give the first round of clues themselves while subsequent rounds will include audience participation. That is, the "audience" asks questions. Continue until one student has correctly completed his/her grid.

Variations:

To make it more challenging:

1. Limit students to two turns, i.e. one turn per flash card. If no one has correctly completed his/her grid, students could then work in pairs or small groups.
2. Have two columns on the answer sheet, rather than a grid, so students will write the names of the students and the vocabulary they are describing.

To make it less challenging:

1. Have students continue giving more clues until everyone has completed their grid.
2. Have students work in small groups or pairs. Give them 15-20 seconds between clues to discuss.

Procedure:

1. Prepare a grid with the terms you want to review.
2. Select student helpers/clue providers to go to the front of the class and give each of them two flashcards.
3. Give the rest of the class the answer grid and tell them to write the student helpers' names.
4. Have student helpers/clue providers give one clue about one of their flashcards in turn. After they have given one clue about each flashcard, the clues should be responses to student questions. (You may want to make rules about the questions they can ask.)
5. Give the class time to think and write between each clue.

6. Students continue giving clues until one student has correctly filled out their grid.

Interesting Story and Questions

Skills: Writing/Reading/Speaking/Listening

Time: 15-30 minutes

Age: 10+

Materials: None

Have students write something interesting. Some examples you can use are: most embarrassing moment, scariest thing you've ever done, your dream for the future, etc. Base it on whatever you are teaching in class. Then, distribute the stories to other people in the class. They have to go around the class, finding the person whose story they have by asking questions. Once they find that person, they have to ask three interesting questions about the story.

Procedure:
1. Have students write an interesting story based on a certain topic. Adjust for length and difficultly depending on your students.
2. Collect stories and redistribute them—one per student, making sure a student does not get their own story.
3. Students go around the class asking people if they have their story. For example, "Did you get in a car accident when you were little?"
4. When they find the person, they must ask them three interesting follow-up questions about it.

Picture Prompt

Skills: Speaking/Listening/Writing

Time: 5 minutes

Age: All

Materials: Picture/PowerPoint image

Show students an image and have them generate questions or speculate about the picture. For lower level students, this can be purely descriptive:
Q: What do you see?
A: I see a house, a car, and some people.
Q: What color is the car?
A: It is blue.

For high beginner/low intermediate students, have an image which can generate questions such as:

- What is happening in this picture?
- How does that person feel?
- Why do you think so?

For more advanced students, have an unusual image. Encourage them to create a narrative to explain the story. This activity can also be done as a Quick Write.

Procedure:

1. In advance, prepare an image, either PowerPoint or a picture large enough for the class to easily see.
2. Divide students into pairs or small groups.

3. Depending on the level of the students:
   - Elicit descriptive sentences about the image. Encourage them to make their own questions to ask a partner.
   - Have them discuss what they think is happening in the picture, how the person/ people feel and why they think so, etc.
   - Have them create a narrative about the image.

Quick Read

Skills: Reading/Writing/Speaking

Time: 10 minutes

Age: All

Materials: Worksheet

Give students a short passage, slightly below their level, and 3-5 comprehension questions. It should be short enough to be completed in 7-8 minutes.

Procedure:
1. Prepare a short passage using language slightly below the class level.
2. Include 3-5 comprehension questions and an example question demonstrating how to answer.
3. Give students 7-8 minutes to read and answer the questions.

Reported Speech

Skills: Writing/Reading/Speaking

Time:

Age: 8+

Materials: None

Optional Materials: Sentence cards, or worksheet/whiteboard/PowerPoint

Reported speech can be difficult for students, so a little regular practice can help make it more automatic.

No materials version: Ask student A a question. Ask student B to "report" student A's answer. Model the activity first by simply asking a student a question and then reporting the answer to the class. Example:

T: What day is it today?

A: Today is Tuesday.

T: A said today is Tuesday.

Procedure:

No materials: Prepare sentences for the students to change to reported speech. Ask one student a question, then ask another to report the answer to the class.

Other variations: Prepare cards/worksheet/PowerPoint or write five sentences on the whiteboard. If using PowerPoint or the whiteboard, have students write their answers in their notebook.

4-Skills: Lower-level

Ball Toss

Skills: Reading/Writing/Speaking/Listening

Time: 5-10 minutes

Age: All

Materials: Lightweight ball (such as a beach ball) with questions written on it

This game has many variations. One variation I have used with great success is writing questions on a beach ball. I use a whiteboard marker to write on the ball, but let it dry thoroughly before class, so it doesn't smudge but it can be washed clean and reused with different questions later. Students gently toss the ball to one another and read aloud and answer the question under their right thumb. A more complex variation is: Student A reads/asks the question, tosses the ball to Student B, who answers that question, then asks the question under their right thumb, and tosses the ball to Student C, who answers Student B's question.

If it's a "getting to know you" activity, use questions to elicit name, age, and basic information. Otherwise, it can be used to practice likes/dislikes, 5 W/H-questions, etc. It is quite a versatile activity and can be used with just about anything that you're studying.

If you don't have a ball handy, you can crumple up a piece of paper to use as a ball. Ask a question and toss the ball to a student. That student must answer and ask a question (the same question for true beginners or related question, if higher level), then toss the "ball" to the next student. If you want the students to ask different questions, you should give them a topic (daily routine, hobbies, etc.) or grammar pattern to use.

If you want to make sure all students have equal turns, have students sit down after catching the ball. If you have more than 10-12 students in your class, you may want to divide them into groups, each with their own ball, so students aren't waiting long periods between turns. This will also increase student talking time.

Procedure:

1. Prepare a beach ball by writing questions on it. Allow enough time for the ink to dry before class. Low prep version: crumple up a piece of scrap paper with the questions written on it.

2. Have students stand in a circle (as much as possible). If your class is large, divide students into groups of 10-12.

Variation A:

When a student catches the ball, they must read out the question under their right thumb. They answer their own question and toss the ball to another student.

Variation B:

When Student A catches the ball, they ask the question under their right thumb to Student B. When Student B answers, A tosses them the ball. Student B asks Student C the question under their right thumb and so on.

No Prep Variation:

The teacher asks a question and tosses the ball to Student A. Student A answers, asks Student B a question, and tosses them the ball.

Categories

Skills: Speaking/Listening/Writing

Time: 5 minutes

Age: All

Materials: None

Optional Materials: Butcher paper/A3 paper

Students can review by brainstorming words they know in a given category, such as food, job, hobbies, etc.

Variation 1: Students work in small groups, making a list of all the words they can think of for that category. The group with the longest list wins.

Variation 2: Students take turns adding one word at a time to the list. If a student repeats a word or says a word which doesn't fit, they are out. This variation is better suited to small classes or groups working independently.

Procedure:

1. Begin by dividing students into groups of 3-5. Small classes can work as a whole.
2. Give each group a piece of A3 or butcher paper. (For a speaking/listening activity, have students take turns adding a word. If students can't add a word, they are out.)
3. Give the class a category, such as jobs or animals and a time limit (about 3 minutes) to brainstorm and write as many words that match the category as possible.
4. The group with the most correct words wins.

Dialogue Substitution

Skills: Reading/Listening/Speaking

Time: 10-15 minutes

Age: 8+

Materials: PowerPoint or handouts of photocopied textbook dialogue with parts removed.

Lower-level text books contain many dialogues but their effectiveness is reduced when students don't have to listen to their partner in order to successfully complete their role. An easy solution to this is to provide the dialogues with key elements missing. Students then have to listen in order to respond appropriately. Dialogues are an excellent way for students to see how new vocabulary is used in real-life situations.

You may want or need to scaffold this activity by providing a list of possible words, phrases, or grammar patterns that could be used to fill the gaps. Alternatively, you can make the activity more difficult or realistic by allowing students to complete the dialogue using any language that makes sense, even if it hasn't been presented in that lesson.

Procedure:

1. Before class, scan or photocopy a textbook dialogue with the target language removed.

2. Optionally, create a list of possible words or phrases that students can use to complete the dialogue or encourage students to use other words or phrases that will fit the target language. Also, introduce any language needed for practicing communication strategies (see above).

3. Divide students into pairs and have them take turns being A and B.

4. To extend the activity, have students change partners and repeat the dialogue, using different words to create a new conversation.

Dictogloss

Skills: Speaking/Listening/Writing

Time: 10-15 minutes

Age: 8+

Materials: A short story

This is a simple activity for higher level students that helps them practice their listening and memory skills, as well as substituting vocabulary words if the original word can no longer be remembered. You can find a short, interesting story of some kind or make up one yourself. I've used various things from children's stories to a story about something I did on the weekend. Just about anything can work.

Tell the story 1-3 times, depending on the student level and of course you can also vary your speaking speed to make this activity easier or harder. Once you are done telling the story, students will have to go in groups of 2-3 to retell the story. Emphasize that they won't be able to recreate the exact story that you told, but that they should try their best to keep the meaning the same. Each team can pair up with another team to compare. Then, tell the original story again so students can see how they did. This activity works well as a writing activity too.

Procedure:

1. Prepare a short story which you'll read to your students.
2. Put students in groups of two or three and read the story to them.
3. Students try to remember the details of the story and compare with their group. I usually only allow them to do this by speaking.
4. Read the story again and students attempt to recreate the story more closely, again by speaking.
5. Read the story again (depending on level and difficulty of story) and

students again attempt to recreate it, even more closely.

6. Elicit a couple of teams to tell their story to the class (in a small class). Or, put two teams together and they tell their stories to each other (in a larger class).

7. Read the story one final time for students to compare their own versions.

-er Dictionary Activity

Skill: Reading/Writing/Speaking/Listening

Time: 10+ minutes

Age: 7+

Materials: Worksheet

Students learn early on that –er refers to a person who does something. Examples include, teacher, writer, baker, etc. However, nouns ending in –er can refer to people, animals, or objects or can have multiple meanings involving a combination of the above. The activity will reinforce the need to be cautious with general rules in English while providing dictionary practice.

Begin by preparing a list of nouns ending with –er. If you would like this to be a brief activity, limit it to about five words. The more words you include, the longer the activity will be. Have three columns beside the list for students to tick if the word refers to a person, animal, and/or object. Students should use their dictionaries to determine which categories each word belongs to.

Here are enough –er words for an entire class period:

Blender, Bumper, Buyer

Cadaver, Canister, Cleaner, Coaster, Customer

Diver, Dozer, Driver

Passenger, Pitcher, Planner, Player

Ringer, Roster

Scanner, Sticker, Stinger

    To add a speaking element, have students work with partners after filling in their answers. Partners should take turns asking and answering questions about the words. For example, "A person who bakes is a baker. Is a person who cooks a cooker?"

Teaching Tips:

    Depending on the level of the class, you can allow students to defend answers they may come up with, such as, "A banner is a person who bans," or simply explain that it is a logical conclusion, but that English is not always logical.

Procedure:

1. Prepare a worksheet with a list of nouns ending in –er with tickbox columns for person, animal, object. Also instruct students to bring their dictionaries on the appropriate date if you do not have class sets.
2. Explain to students that although they know that nouns ending in –er are people, -er words can also refer to animals and objects.

3. Have students use their dictionaries to categorize each word on the list as person, animal, and/or object.

4. When students have looked up all the words, have them work with a partner asking and answering questions about the words. For example, "Is a walker a person who walks?"

Is that Sentence Correct?

Skills: Listening/Speaking/Reading/Writing

Time: 10-20 minutes

Age: All

Materials: Blank paper, vocabulary words

This is a sneaky way to get your students to make grammatically correct sentences using the target vocabulary. Start off by giving your students 5-6 vocabulary words. They should be words that the students are quite familiar with already. The challenge in this activity is not the actual word; it's using it in a sentence. Give the students five minutes to make some sentences using those words (one sentence per word). Do not offer any assistance or correct any errors. You can also make some sentences using the same (or different, but familiar to the student) vocabulary words. Some of them should be correct while some of them should be incorrect.

The first student reads his/her first sentence. Discuss whether it is correct or incorrect and why. Read your first sentence and have a brief discussion about whether it is correct or incorrect. The activity continues until all the sentences are done. If you have a larger class (more than six students), you can put students into groups of 3-4 and have them make sentences together.

Procedure:

1. Give the students a few vocabulary words (and, as the teacher, you can use the same words or different words that the students are familiar with).
2. Instruct the students to write one sentence per word while you do the same with your words. Make some sentences correct and some incorrect.
3. Take turns reading sentences and discussing whether they are correct or incorrect.

Q&A

Skills: Speaking/Listening/Reading/Writing

Time: 10 minutes

Age: 7+

Materials: None

This is a simple variation on having students make example sentences using their vocabulary list. Students work in pairs of teams, creating a list of WH questions (to avoid yes/no answers) using their vocabulary words. When they have five questions, teams should alternate asking questions to another team and answering the other team's questions.

You can extend the activity with some reported speech practice, which will give teams an incentive to listen to the responses to their questions.

Procedure:
1. Divide students into an even number of teams of 2-4. Then pair two teams together.
2. Give students a few minutes to create five WH questions using their vocabulary words.
3. Have paired teams alternate asking and answering questions.

Role-Plays

Skills: Writing/Reading/Speaking/Listening

Time Required: 20-40 minutes

Age: 10+

Materials: None

Partner role-plays are an excellent way to get students practicing using new vocabulary in a real-life context. Give the students a conversation starter to get them going. For example, if you're talking about *feelings* in class that day, you can use:

A: Hey _____, how are you doing?

B: I'm great, how are you?

A: I'm _____ (sad, embarrassed, angry, bored, etc.). ***Anything besides, "I'm fine, thank you, and you?" is good. ***

B: Oh? What's wrong?

A: _____.

B: _____.

Another context that I often use this activity with is *illness or injury*. For example:

A: Hey _____, you don't look (sound) so good! What's wrong?

B: Oh yeah, I'm not good. I _____.

A: Really? _____.

B: _____.

A: _____.

One final context that I use this with is *excuses*. For example:

A: Hey _____, you're _____ minutes late!

B: I'm really sorry. I've been/I had to _____.

A: Hmmm . . . _____.

Give students about ten minutes to write the conversation with their partner. You can adjust the number of lines and how detailed of a starter you give to suit the ability level of your students. For lower-level students, it can be helpful to have a word bank relevant to the context on the whiteboard so that the writing portion of this activity doesn't get too long (you can also provide them with a detailed, fill-in-the-blank script). Then, the students memorize their conversation (no papers when speaking!), and do a role-play in front of their classmates if you have a small class of fewer than ten.

Teaching Tips:

Having students make conversations is very useful for practicing functional language and speaking sub-skills. I usually choose one or two functions to mention when I'm giving the instructions for the activity and provide a bit of coaching and language input surrounding that, depending on the level—

beginners will need more help.

The functions that fit particularly well with partner conversations include agreeing, disagreeing, apologizing, and asking advice. The sub-skills that you can emphasize are things like turn-taking, initiating a conversation, speaking for an appropriate length of time, stress and intonation, responding (really?), and cohesive devices, particularly noun pronoun reference: A: I saw a <u>movie</u> last night. B: Which <u>one</u> did you see? A. I saw <u>Iron Man.</u> It was good.

This is one of the most useful things you can do in your conversation classes, especially for beginner or intermediate students so make sure you try it out at least once or twice over the course of a semester. It gives your students a chance to have a real conversation which will build a lot of confidence, but they won't have the pressure of coming up with something to say on the spot.

Procedure:
1. Prepare a conversation starter based on what you are teaching.
2. (Optional) Pre-teach some language that students could use, if you haven't done that already in your lesson.
3. Write the conversation starter on the whiteboard, PowerPoint, or on a handout.
4. Have students complete the conversation in pairs. Then, they must prepare to speak by memorizing and adding in stress and intonation. You could give some individual help to each pair to assist them in knowing what to stress and how to do it.
5. Have students stand up and "perform" their conversation if you have a

small class. In larger classes, there are a few other options (see above).

6. Reward teams for interesting conversations, good acting (no reading), and correct use of grammar/vocabulary that you were teaching that day.

Running Dictation

Skills: Writing/Listening/Speaking/Reading

Time: 15 minutes

Age: 8+

Materials: The "dictation" + some way to attach it to the walls or board.

This is one of my favorite activities which covers reading, writing, listening and speaking. There are a wide variety of English styles you can choose: poems, song lyrics, a short story, famous quotes—the list is almost limitless. For example, you might make up a story or conversation a few sentences long (no more than ten). Put each sentence on a strip of paper, and you can also put another strip of paper on top to prevent cheating. Put these around the classroom in various locations.

The students will be in teams of two. One person is the reader and one is the writer. The reader gets up and reads a bit of the passage and comes and tells it to the writer. They go back to remember more of it and so on and so on. At the end, the students have to put the song or conversation in order. If you have beginner students, make sure it's obvious enough what the correct order should be. Intermediate and advanced students can handle something with a bit of ambiguity. When they're done, I'll check their writing and if there aren't many mistakes plus the order is correct, that team is the winner. How many mistakes you allow depends on the level of your students.

Tell your students before the activity starts that standing at the strip of paper and then yelling to their partner instead of walking over to them is not allowed or they will be disqualified.

Teaching Tips:

Make sure you let your students know what cheating is (yelling, the "reader/speaker" touching the pen, using their phone camera) and if that happens their team will automatically be disqualified.

Procedure:

1. Prepare a simple story or conversation and put each sentence on a strip of paper.
2. Put the papers around the classroom on the wall, equally spaced out.
3. Divide the students into pairs: one writer and one reader.
4. The reader stands up, walks to the station and reads a paper, then goes back to the writer and tells what they read to the writer, who must write it. The reader can go back to a single paper as many times as required.
5. This procedure of reading, speaking, listening, and writing continues until the team has all the sentences down on their paper.
6. The two students put the story or conversation in the correct order.
7. The teacher can check for accuracy and meaning and decide if it's acceptable, or not.

Sentence Substitution Ladder

Skills: Speaking/Listening/Writing (optional)

Time: 5-20 minutes

Age: 8+

Materials: Sentences

This is a simple activity to get students to think about how they can use the words they know. They will be very familiar with substitution drills, but this goes one step further to get lower-level students comfortable with using the language a bit more creatively. They have the knowledge, but they may need a push to use it.

Give the class a sentence practicing familiar categories of words (places, activities, etc.) and a familiar grammatical structure. Then, instruct him/her to change one word at a time to make a new sentence. Each position must be changed one time (as in, first word, second word, etc.), but it doesn't have to be done in order. Optionally, you can have them write the new sentences.

An example ladder would be:

Original sentence: I saw a black cat walk under a ladder.

I saw an orange cat walk under a ladder.

We saw an orange cat walk under a ladder.

We saw an orange cat run under a ladder.

We saw an orange cat run under the bed.

We saw an orange cat run to the bed.

Procedure:
1. In advance, prepare several sentences using familiar categories of words (places, activities, etc.) and a familiar grammatical structure.
2. Have the students change one word at a time to make a new sentence.
3. Each position must be changed one time (as in, first word, second word, etc.), but it doesn't have to be done in order.

Word Association

Skills: Reading/Writing/Listening/Speaking

Time: 5 minutes

Age: 7+

Materials: whiteboard and markers or butcher (A3) paper and pens

To introduce a new vocabulary word, write it in the middle of the board or paper and have students take turns adding as many words or images related to that word as possible. For large classes, have students work in groups with separate pieces of paper taped to the wall or the top of the table/grouped desks. After a given amount of time (2-3 minutes, or when you see no one is adding anything new), discuss their answers.

Procedure:
1. Write a single new vocabulary word on the whiteboard or butcher paper.
2. Have students take turns adding as many words or images related to that word as possible.
3. After 2-3 minutes (or less, if no one is adding anything new), discuss their answers.

Speaking & Listening: Higher-level

120-90-60 Fluency Activity

Skills: Speaking/Listening

Time: 15 minutes

Age: 10+

Materials: None

If you want to help your students speak more quickly and fluently, this is the perfect ESL speaking activity for you. Give your students a topic that they know a lot about. For example: good or bad points about their school or hometown. I often give half the students one topic and the other half another just to make it a bit more interesting to listen to. Give your students 3-5 minutes to prepare, depending on their level. But, emphasize that they should just write one or two words for each point, and not full sentences because it is actually a speaking activity and not a writing one.

Then, with a partner, the first student has to give their speech and talk continuously for two minutes, while their partner listens. I use an online stopwatch so that the students can see the clock count down. Then, I give the students another two minutes and they switch roles.

After that, the students have to find a new partner and the activity repeats, except they have to include ALL the same information as before, just in 90 seconds. Then, switch again, with 60 more seconds. One way that you can help your students make the transition to less time is by giving them 30 seconds between rounds to think about how to say something more concisely, go over in their head the part of their speech where they had to slow down for some reason or to think about where they could use conjunctions.

You could give an example of something like this: "I like watching The Simpsons. It's funny. It's interesting. My mother, father, brother and I watch while we're eating dinner almost every night of the week" --->"I like watching The Simpsons because it's funny and interesting. I watch with my family almost every night while eating dinner. "

For lower level students, you can adjust the times to make them shorter and easier because talking for two minutes can be quite difficult.

Emphasize that students must include all of the key information even though they have less time to say it. Speak more quickly or more concisely!

Procedure:

1. Give students a topic and some time to prepare their "speech."
2. Students give their speech to a partner, talking for two minutes without stopping. Switch roles and the second student gives their speech.
3. Students find a new partner and give their speech again, this time in 90 seconds. Switch roles.
4. Students find a new partner and give their in 60 seconds. Switch roles.

20 Questions

Skills: Speaking/Listening

Time: 20 minutes

Age: 8+

Materials: None

This is a "20 questions" style game based on whatever you're studying such as animals or jobs that is particularly effective for working on yes/no question forms and also logical thinking. If you have higher level students, this works well as a warm-up or icebreaker activity. You can leave it open and allow the students to choose any person, place or thing. The teacher starts the game by thinking of a secret thing and the students can ask the teacher yes/no questions. Keep track of how many questions are asked and incorrect answers count as a guess too. Students can then play the game in small groups or in pairs, which will significantly increase the student talking time.

Teaching Tips:

It is especially important to do a demonstration of this game because in my experience, it isn't played in many parts of the world. You can also coach students a little bit on what good and bad questions types are, such as a guess right at the start of the game is a terrible as is a too specific type of question, but a general question which eliminates a lot of possible answers is a good one (animals: Does it have 4 legs?", or jobs: "Do I need to go to university to get it?").

This game is easily adaptable to make it much easier or much more difficult. To make it very difficult, just say that the secret word has to be a noun. If you want to make it less difficult, specify either a person, place or thing. Finally, the easiest version is to choose a more specific category such as animals or jobs. If you choose the easiest version, you might want to reduce the number of questions from 20 down to 10. For absolute beginners, it's useful to write some example questions on the board for them to refer to throughout the activity.

This is another one of those absolutely nothing required in the way of preparation or materials games which can be played with a variety of levels and class sizes (from 1-40). Keep it in your bag of tricks to pull out in case of emergency.

Procedure:
1. The teacher chooses a secret thing for the example. Students ask a yes/no question. The teacher answers the question and puts one tick (checkmark) on the board.
2. Students ask more questions and the game continues until the students either guess the secret thing or they reach 20 questions/guesses. If you have a small class, it's easy to monitor the activity to ensure that each student gets to ask a question. If you have a larger class, you can make a rule that once a student has asked one question, they cannot ask another one until five more questions have been asked. If the students guess the secret thing, they win. If they reach 20 questions without guessing, the teacher is the winner.

3. Each guess also counts as one question, in order to prevent random guessing.
4. Students can play the game in partners or small groups of 3-5. Whoever guesses the correct answer gets to choose the next secret thing.

Celebrity Talk Show

Skills: Listening/Speaking

Time: 10-15 minutes

Age: 10+

Materials: None

Optional Materials: Toy microphones; video clip with monitor

This is more like a presentation activity, in that not all students will be a celebrity each time the activity is done. Rather, it is spread across the term. This activity helps students think a bit more deeply about the stories they read and connect with the characters.

The "celebrities" are actually characters from a story we've read, as well as the author. In the talk show format, each is interviewed in turn by a student host, followed by questions from the audience.

Before beginning the activity, it's helpful to discuss what talk shows they've seen, and questions that usually get asked. If possible, show a short clip from a talk show. Have them think about the particular story they have read in order to ask more relevant questions, rather than the same generic questions each time.

For example, "How did you feel when _____ happened?" or, "Why did you do _____?"

Procedure:

1. Before class, set up a desk and two chairs, talk show-style.

2. To demonstrate, find a short clip of a popular celebrity being interviewed on a talk show to show the class, or simply explain about talk shows: what kinds of questions are asked, etc.

3. Choose two students to play interviewer/host and guest. You should keep track of who has had a turn, so each student gets to participate over the term.

4. Have the pair come to the front of the class (the audience) and hold their interview. The guests will play a story character or author.

5. After a set number of questions (about 5) or your time limit, open the floor to questions from the audience. Ask your own questions, if the audience doesn't ask many of their own.

Five-Minute Debate

Skills: Speaking/Listening
Time: 10 minutes
Age: 10+
Materials: None

Give students an age-appropriate controversial statement. If you are knowledgeable about pop culture, you can start with, "so and so is the best X (singer, soccer player, whatever)," if your students are too young for truly controversial topics. In pairs or small groups, have them debate the sides. You may have to assign sides, if too many agree or disagree with your premise.

You may need to scaffold with language like, "I think ____, because ____." "I agree with X, but ____."

Procedure:
1. Divide students into pairs or small groups.
2. Give students a controversial statement. I would prepare this in advance, focusing on a recent news item or pop culture, but you could probably think of something on the fly if you needed something on the spot.
3. Give students a time limit to discuss the merits of their side, trying to change the mind of their "opponent".
4. If necessary, begin with some helpful language, such as, "I feel ___, because ___."
5. Finish with a quick poll to see if anyone changed their side.

If I Had a Million Dollars

Skills: Listening/speaking

Time: 10+ minutes

Age: 10+

Materials: AV equipment for song/video

This is an activity you can use to discuss hypothetical situations and to focus on conditionals. If you wish, you can start by playing the Barenaked Ladies song or video of the same name. Then, tell the students that there is a big Lotto draw coming up, you have a ticket and are thinking about what you'll do if you win. Give them several ideas of what you would do with a million dollars.

If you have the students work in pairs or small groups, the activity will be fairly short, although you can lengthen it a bit by announcing to the class some of the more creative ideas you hear—encouraging them to think beyond mansions and luxury cars. To extend the game further, have students regroup themselves every few minutes. At the end, you can ask students to share the best ideas they heard.

If you want to challenge your advanced level students, find the song lyrics, cut and paste them into a worksheet, but omit some of the vocabulary words and get students to fill in the blanks as they listen to the song. I find that one out of every 15-20 words is a good rule of thumb.

Procedure:

1. Play the Barenaked Ladies song. I used a *YouTube* version with lyrics. Optionally, have students fill in a worksheet with some of the song lyric words omitted.

2. Set up the scenario for students: a big Lotto drawing is coming up and you

have a ticket. Give them several ideas of what you would do if you won.

3. Divide students into small groups and discuss what they would do if they won a million dollars.

4. To extend the activity, regroup students every few minutes.

Just a Minute

Skills: Speaking

Time: 5-10 minutes

Age: 8+

Materials: whiteboard, timer

This is a very simple activity that you can use as a fast warm-up at the beginning of class in order to get your students talking. Write a bunch of general categories on the board such as jobs, hobbies, dreams, movies, food, etc. Put the students into groups of 4 and they can number themselves 1-2-3-4. Then, ask one of the students to throw a paper airplane at the board and whatever word it gets closest to is the topic for the first student. All the number ones must talk about that topic for one minute without stopping and if they stop or have a long pause, they've lost the challenge. You can adjust the time limit to be higher or lower depending on the level of students (beginner = 30 seconds, advanced = 2 minutes). Erase the first speaking round word from the board and continue the activity with the remaining three students except that they have different topics. It's helpful if the teacher does an example speech first with a topic that the students choose.

Procedure:

1. The teacher writes topics on the whiteboard (teacher-supplied, or elicited from students).
2. Put students into groups of 4. They number themselves 1-2-3-4.
3. The teacher does an example speech with a topic that students choose.
4. One student throws a paper airplane at the whiteboard. The topic closest to where it hits is the first one.
5. Student one has to talk about that topic for a minute without stopping. The goal is to have minimal pauses and to never stop talking. (Optional: the other three students each ask a follow-up question).
6. Erase the first speaking round word. Another student throws the paper airplane and finds another topic. The number two students talk for a minute. Continue with the third and fourth rounds' students.

Me, Too!

Skills: Speaking/Listening

Time: 5-10 minutes

Age: 6+

Materials: None

This is a simple activity to uncover what your students have in common with one another. If possible, arrange the seats in a circle, so everyone can see each other. Begin by sharing a fact about yourself that you don't think is unique or unusual. For example, "I like to hike in my free time." Any students in the class who also enjoy hiking should stand (or raise their hands) and say, "Me, too!" Go around the circle and have each student share one fact about themselves. You could extend the activity by keeping track of numbers and noting which facts are common to the most number of students.

Teaching Tips:

You may need to remind them that these are not unusual facts; these should be things they expect to have in common with at least one other person.

Procedure:

1. If possible, arrange the seats in a circle.
2. Begin by sharing a fact about yourself that you don't think is unique or unusual. For example, "I like to hike in my free time."
3. Ask any students in the class who also enjoy hiking to stand (or raise their hands) and say, "Me, too!"
4. Go around the circle and have each student share one fact about themselves.
5. You could extend the activity by keeping track of numbers and noting which facts are common to the most number of students.

Round Robin Story

Skills: Listening/Speaking

Time: 10 minutes

Age: 7+

Materials: whiteboard, marker

This activity is easy, low prep, and doesn't require any materials. To begin, have the students sit in a large circle. Start them off with a "Once upon a time ____" sentence. Say it as well as write it on the whiteboard.

The story then builds as it travels around the room. Each student adds one sentence, which you write (with any mistakes corrected) on the board. This is not a memory game—students only need to add a new sentence which continues the story, rather than repeat it from the beginning. It should, however, make sense in the context of the story.

When all students have added a sentence, you can either add a sentence to end it, if necessary, or ask for volunteers to finish the story. Then, the entire class can read the story aloud from the board. If you have not written it on the board, you can retell or summarize it.

Procedure:

1. Have students sit in a large circle, if possible.
2. Begin with a "Once upon a time" sentence. Say it and write it on the whiteboard.
3. Have the student closest to you add a sentence and the teacher writes it (correctly) on the board.
4. Continue around the room, until everyone has added a sentence or two.
5. Add a sentence to end the story, or have volunteers finish it.

Story Picture Cards Sequencing

Skills: Speaking/Listening

Time: 15+ minutes

Age: 10+

Materials: Laminated cards which have a sequence of pictures, one per student plus your own

This is an activity better suited to higher level students. In advance, prepare individual pictures which tell a story when put together. Give each student one picture. Without showing one another their pictures, students must discuss the images in order to determine the correct sequence of images which tells a story. When they think they have the correct order, everyone reveals their pictures to see if they are correct.

Teaching Tips:

If the class is very large, have two or even three different sets of pictures, each telling a different story. Clearly mark each set, so students know who they should be working with. This is intended to be a mingling activity, but it could be done in groups while sitting.

Make sure the pictures have elements which lend themselves to easier sequencing, such as a clock, the sun/moon, and activities usually done at a certain time, such as eating, commuting, and working.

The books Zoom and Re-Zoom by Istvan Banyai are perfect for this activity, if you can get your hands on a copy. Just be sure to use a sequence of pages in order.

Procedure:
1. Prepare a series of pictures which tell a story when put in order.
2. Tell students they must discuss their pictures without revealing them to each other, in order to determine the correct sequence of the images.
3. When the students all think they have the correct order, have them reveal their pictures to one another to see if they are correct. The teacher can check answers with the class if necessary.

Talking Bag

Skills: Speaking/Listening

Time: 5-10 minutes

Age: 8+

Materials: Questions cards, bag/box/bowl

Procedure:

In advance, prepare a bag (or box, bowl, etc) full of question cards (laminate them!)

Variation 1: Draw a question from the bag and read/write it. Have students ask and answer the question with the person next to them.

Variation 2: Choose one student to draw a question. That student asks the question to one other student, who then draws a question to ask a third student. Before beginning, set a time limit or decide how many students will have a turn.

Variation 3: Divide students into small groups of 3-5. Have one member of each group draw one question to ask, and have each group member take turns answering.

Speaking & Listening: Lower-level

Basketball Vocabulary Challenge

Skills: Listening/Speaking

Time: 10-15 minutes

Age: 7+

Materials: Empty trash can, "balls"

    This is a fun game that children love! You can play with the entire class if you have fewer than eight students or in teams if you have more, but you need a big space to play it, such as a large classroom with few desks, gymnasium or outside. Place the empty trash can in the middle of the open space. Arrange the students around the room as far from the basket as possible (touching the wall, behind the chalk line, etc.) and give each student a ball. They can be real balls, but I find that a piece of scrunched up scrap paper works best. Then, place a line of flashcards in front of each person leading toward the basket. Five per player works well.

    Going in order one student at a time; the students have two choices: aim for the basket, or say the vocabulary word on the flashcard immediately in front of them and move up closer to the basket. If they aim for the basket but miss, they are out of the game and must go sit down. If they say the word correctly, they move up closer and wait until the next round when they have the same decision. If they say the wrong word, they are also out of the game. Continue in a circle until all the players are out of the game, either because they missed a shot, got a shot in the basket or said a vocabulary word incorrectly. You can give a point or small prize to the first player to get a shot in the basket.

An optional variation is to give different points for various shots as you would in a regular basketball game. For example, from flashcards #5/4 = 3 points. Flashcards #3/2 = 2 points. Flashcard #1 = 1 point.

Procedure:

1. Place an empty trash cash in the center of a large playing area.
2. Arrange five flashcards per student leading from the perimeter to the basket.
3. Line students up at the perimeter behind a row of flashcards. Each student has to be holding a ball of some kind.
4. Students take turns in order and have two choices. The first choice is to shoot their ball at the basket. If they miss, they are out of the game. If they make the basket, they get a point. The other choice is to say the word on the flashcard closest to them and if correct, they move up to that location and waits until their next turn. If incorrect, they are out of the game.
5. The winner is the first student(s) to score a basket. Or, if you're giving different points for the various shots, you can play 3-5 rounds and add up the scores from each round.

Board Games

Skills: Reading/Speaking

Time: 25-40 minutes

Age: 6+

Materials: Board game sheet and token for each student (a coin or eraser)

Board Games often come in the "teacher's resource book" that goes along with your textbook and if this is the case, you're in luck because no preparation will be required, but you'll have a solid activity that your students will probably love and it has the added bonus of being extremely student-centered. However, don't worry if there isn't a pre-made game in the textbook because it's easier than you might think to make your own. It will only take 5-10 minutes once you get a bit of experience doing it.

Use questions based on the grammar and/or vocabulary that you've been studying during the previous classes. Have some fun squares, such as, "Switch positions with the person on your right" or, "Go back 5 spaces." The style I typically use is a question of some kind where the student has to speak one or two sentences in response to it. The other students in the group listen for incorrect answers, in which case the student has to move back the number that they "rolled." You can use dice (which gets loud), two coins (2 heads = 5, 1 head + 1 tail = 3, 2 tails = 1), or a number sheet where students close their eyes and move their pen to choose a number.

Procedure:

1. Hand out the "game boards" as well as dice or coins to groups of 3-5

students. Have each student provide their own token—it can be an eraser, a key or a small piece of paper.
2. The students can do rock-scissor-paper to see who goes first. The first student uses the dice or coins to find the number of spaces they will move ahead. That student answers the question and if correct, they stay on that space but if incorrect, they move back the number of spaces that they rolled.
3. The next student rolls the dice and answers a question and so on.
4. The game continues until one student reaches the final square on the game.

Bumbling Blindfold

Skills: Speaking/Listening

Time: 20 minutes

Age: 8+

Materials: Blindfold

If you're studying about directions (go straight, left, right, turn-around, stop, etc.) this is a really fun activity. Blindfold one student and put them at the starting point. The other students have to give them directions so they can get to the finish point without bumping into anything. Be sure to move anything that students could walk into and hurt themselves with. Also caution them that they need to walk slowly and that if they run, they will have to sit down and their turn will be over.

Procedure:
1. Have one student wait outside the class for a minute.
2. Show remaining students the start and the finish point.
3. Go outside and blindfold the student and lead him into the classroom.
4. The other students must give him directions to get from the starting point to the finish point.

Chain Spelling

Skills: Speaking/listening
Time: 5 minutes
Age: 6+
Materials: None

If you want to practice spelling some vocab words that you're been studying, use this game. Have all the students stand up and the teacher says a word. The first student says the first letter, the next student the next letter, and on and on. If someone makes a mistake, they sit down and you start with the next student and new word. Continue until you have only 1 or 2 students standing. This is an excellent "filler" game if you have a few minutes left-over at the end of class—just use whatever vocabulary you had been studying that day.

Teaching Tip:

Spelling is an often neglected skill in many classrooms but it's an important one. I now teach academic writing at a major university in South Korea and some students have atrocious spelling which really hampers their ability to write well. Nobody will take you seriously, no matter how good your ideas are if you make basic spelling mistakes.

Procedure:

1. All students stand up.
2. The teacher says a word.
3. The first student must say the first letter.
4. The next student must say the second letter, etc.
5. If incorrect, the student has to sit down. The teacher says a new word and the game continues until there are only one or two students remaining.

Charades with Speaking

Skills: Speaking

Time: 20-30 minutes

Age: 6+

Materials: whiteboard

You can use this activity to review whatever vocabulary you're teaching (verbs work especially well). Write down some words or phrases that can be easily acted out on small pieces of paper and put them in an envelope.

Divide the class into two teams. The first team sends one person (the captain) up to the front and he/she has to act out and describe in English as many things as possible in two minutes. Alternatively, you can have each team member rotate through the captain role during a single 3-4 minute round. The first person describes the first word and after his/her team guesses it, then he/she can go to the back of the line and the next person comes up. Then, the next team will go. You can do as many rounds as you want with different captains.

Teaching Tips:

To add even more fun, if there is a team that is behind by a lot of points you can have a double and then a triple bonus round to give them some hope that they can catch up and maybe even win.

Procedure:

1. Prepare some words or phrases beforehand, based on whatever you're teaching.
2. Divide the class into two teams and each team can choose its first captain.
3. Team A sends its captain to the front and he/she randomly chooses a paper and must describe and act it out.
4. Team A must then guess what the captain is describing. When the team guesses correctly, the captain takes another word and the game continues. Alternatively, you can have the students rotate the captain role amongst themselves during the course of a single round. In this case, make the round a bit longer—maybe four minutes instead of two.
5. Each round is 2-4 minutes and each team tries to get as many words as possible.
6. The other teams goes next and uses different words.
7. You can play as many rounds as you want, but make sure you have different captains for each one so everyone gets a chance to describe the words.

Deserted Island

Skills: Speaking/Listening

Time: 5-10 minutes

Age: 8+

Materials: None

Deserted Island is an excellent way to uncover what things are most important to students. Tell students that there is a terrible storm and their ship is sinking, but thankfully, they can bring three objects with them. It doesn't need to be realistic or necessary for survival, just something that they want to have with them during their time on the island. Encourage creativity and imagination. Then, have students share their answers with the class (if under ten students), or in small groups (in larger classes), and give a reason why they'd bring each item.

Procedure:

1. Tell students that they are on a ship and it's sinking. Thankfully, there is an island nearby that is already well-stocked with everything they'll need for survival.

2. Each student has to choose three things that they'd like to have with them during their time on the island. It doesn't need to be realistic or necessary for survival.

3. Students share their answers and why they chose each item with the class (if under ten students), or in small groups (in larger classes).

Draw a Picture, but Someone Else is Talking

Skills: Speaking/Listening

Time: 10-15 minutes

Age: 7+

Materials: Blank paper

This is a fun way to practice body parts or descriptive words (big, small, long, etc.) and I guarantee that everyone will be laughing throughout this activity. The students sit back to back and one person is the "talker" while the other one is the "drawer." The person talking describes something that they're looking at to their partner (a face, a body, a city, a monster) and that person draws what they hear. The results are usually hilarious and fun to show to the rest of the class!

Teaching Tips:

Some useful functional language that you can practice with this activity is asking for clarification. You can pre-teach some language surrounding the topic, such as:

How _____ (long, tall, etc.)?

What do you mean?

I didn't understand, could you say it again?

What did you say? I couldn't hear you.

This activity can get quite loud so it's best to ask students to spread out in the classroom, if possible.

If you teach absolute beginners this is also a great activity, but you might have to do it in a more teacher-centered way. For example, the students could describe a picture to you that you draw on the board, or you could describe something to them and they all draw their own versions of it.

Procedure:
1. Two students sit back to back but close enough to talk to each other.
2. Give student A a picture of some kind, based on whatever you are studying. I usually put something up on the PowerPoint and have the drawer sit with their back towards the screen.
3. Student A describes the picture to student B who must draw it, without looking at the original picture. Student B can ask some questions to student A to clarify if necessary.
4. Compare the original picture with the drawing and laugh a lot!

English Central

Skills: Listening/Speaking

Time: 10-15 minutes

Age: 6+

Materials: Internet connection

English Central (www.englishcentral.com/videos) is YouTube for language learners. There is premium content and functionality, but you can enjoy many features for free. YouTube, of course, has subtitles on some videos, but English Central takes it to the next level. First, the videos are intended for use with students, so they have been curated and organized by level, topic and/or language skill. Each video is segmented for easy replay of a chunk of speech.

Students can also click on a single word to hear it pronounced slowly and learn the definition.

Pronunciation is one activity you can use English Central for with your students. Have them listen to a clip and repeat. You can pause after each phrase or sentence and repeat as needed.

Procedure:
1. In advance, make sure you will have an Internet connection.
2. Either select a video in advance or let your students choose one. There are "courses" that are sets of related videos, that you can work through in a series.
3. Play the clip once or twice first so the students can hear the entire thing.
4. Play one segment (sentence or phrase) at a time and have the students repeat, trying to copy the pronunciation.
5. End by watching the entire clip one more time and discussing and/or summarizing.

"Find Someone Who _____" Bingo

Skills: Speaking/Listening/Writing

Time: 10-15 minutes

Age: 8+

Materials: Blank "Bingo" grids or blank paper

Optional Materials: PowerPoint or whiteboard and marker

This is a good icebreaker to help students get to know one another or to practice asking and answering questions about likes/dislikes, future plans, hobbies, etc. If I have my own classroom, I keep a stack of blank grids handy, but if I'm moving from class to class, I tend to have students use their notebooks.

To save time, I prepare a PowerPoint with possible items to complete the Bingo grid, such as a list of hobbies, jobs, places, etc.—whatever topics you want to include. If I'm using this as an icebreaker, I may list hobbies, musical instruments, and popular films or games so students may learn that one student plays the cello while another likes math.

Rather than have a Bingo caller, students must circulate around the class and ask each other questions to mark out items on their grid. For example, if the topic is jobs, they could ask, "What job do you want?" I have them write the other student's name in the grid, rather than simply cross it out. So, if a student says, "Doctor," they will write that student's name in that block. Before you begin, give them a target of one line, etc. to get Bingo.

I encourage students to move around by only allowing each name to be used once per board in a large class. If the class is quite small, two to three times on a 5x5 grid may be necessary. The goal is to have students practicing the target language, rather than standing with one person and saying, "Do you like apples? Oranges? Bananas? Pears? Melons? Bingo!"

Procedure:

1. Optional: prepare Bingo grid cards and a PowerPoint with questions before class. Otherwise, have students use notebook paper. Tell them what size grid to draw: 3x3, 4x4, or 5x5.

2. Have students fill in their grid with items from the PPT or whiteboard, or create their own, according to a given topic, such as hobbies or likes/dislikes.

3. Have students mingle and ask questions to match students to their grid spaces. For example, student A asks, "Do you like apples?" If student B answers, "Yes, I do," student A writes their name in the "apples" box and moves to the next student.

4. The first student to get a Bingo by finding different students to complete their grid is the winner.

Flashcard Sentences

Skills: Speaking
Time: 5-10 Minutes
Age: 6-8
Materials: Flashcards

You can use this for whatever grammar and vocab points you're studying. Go around the room asking each student or pair a question. Pull a flashcard from your pile and then the student has to make a sentence using the grammar point with that card. A correct sentence gets the card; not correct, and the card goes back at the bottom of the pile. The winner is the person or the team with the most points.

Teaching Tip:

This works best in small classes of eight or smaller. If you have bigger classes, it's possible to put students in groups of four and have two teams of two competing against each other. You can act as the referee if required.

Procedure:

1. Get a flashcard from your pile.
2. Ask one student or pair to make a sentence with that card.
3. If correct, the student keeps the card.
4. If incorrect, the flashcard goes to the bottom of the pile. Continue until the cards are gone or the time is up.

Hidden Object Pictures

Skill: Speaking

Time: 10-15+ minutes

Age: 6+

Materials: Worksheet, crayons or markers

You may remember hidden object pictures from your childhood. While they may seem a bit juvenile, coloring is currently quite trendy, and your students may get a kick out of this. If you have some Photoshop skills, you could alter an "adult" coloring page to fit this activity.

If you haven't done this before, it is a drawing with a number of objects "hidden" in the picture. Obviously, it is best suited to teaching nouns. Students should work in pairs or small groups, discussing the picture as they look for the list of objects. In any case, you don't want your students to sit silently for an entire class period coloring.

Teaching Tips:

If you want to make sure each person has a fairly equal amount of speaking practice, give each member of the group a part of the list. This will force students to ask each other what objects are on the other lists.

If you decide to have students color, then you don't need a full set of crayons or markers for each student. Put two complete sets in baskets or cups for each table to share.

Procedure:

1. In advance, prepare a hidden object picture worksheet (there are many available for free online) and, optionally, bring sufficient crayons or markers for the class.

2. Begin with a brief review of the vocabulary related to the hidden items.

3. Divide students into groups of 2-4 and have them work together to find the hidden images.

4. Finish by having students show their pictures and naming the images they have found. You can extend the task by having students describe the main image, as well.

Hot Potato

Skills: Speaking

Time: 5-10 minutes

Age: 6+

Materials: Flashcards, timer, "potato" (an object for students to pass around)

This is a simple vocabulary review game, spiced up with a timer. There are plenty of phone app timers, but a kitchen timer works well. To play, start the potato, which can be a whiteboard eraser, ball, or any lightweight, easily-seen object, moving around the class from student to student. If there is not a practical way to play in a circle, have a contingency for the last student getting the potato back to the first student, such as pausing the timer.

When the timer goes off, the student holding the potato is shown a flash card. If they can correctly identify the word, they stay alive, but if they are wrong, they are out and must sit down. Vary the length of time for the timer, generally 5-15 seconds, with an occasional longer or shorter spell.

A variation is to have two potatoes which look different. The person holding potato A must ask the person holding potato B a question about the flash card, and that student must answer. For example:

A: Do you like oranges?

B: Yes, I do/No, I don't.

Teaching Tip:

If the class is large, this can be a very long game and the students who are out will lose interest quickly. So, I would break large classes into groups of 10-15. All groups use the same timer and flash card—I simply say, "Three, two, one," and the students holding potatoes all say their answers together.

Procedure:

1. If possible, move students into a circle. Simply have them stand around the edge of the classroom. If the class is very large, divide into groups of 10-15 and make the appropriate number of circles.

2. Begin moving a "potato" around the circle.

3. Set a timer for a random (brief) amount of time. Five to fifteen seconds is good, with an occasional shorter or longer time.

4. When the timer goes off, show a flash card (or PowerPoint image).

5. The student holding the potato must correctly identify the image or sit down. If playing with more than one group, count 3, 2, 1, and have them answer together.

6. The winner is the last person standing.

I'm an Alien

Skills: Speaking/listening

Time: 5-15 minutes

Age: All

Materials: None

I love a no-prep, no-materials activity, and students generally enjoy this one. You begin class by telling the students you are an alien. You landed just a few minutes earlier, right outside the school. Since you are new here, you don't know a lot of words, and you need some help.

You can create a mission scenario, and elicit vocabulary that will help you. Maybe you want to send a letter telling your mother you arrived safely. You can elicit pen, paper, stamp, envelope, post office. Maybe you need to meet someone in another part of the school, such as the cafeteria. You can elicit types of rooms in a school (hall, bathroom, library, etc.) as well as direction words.

Procedure:
1. Begin class by telling the students you are an alien. Since you are new here, you don't know a lot of words, and you need some help.
2. Create a mission scenario, and elicit vocabulary that will help you complete it. For example, you want to send a letter telling your mother you arrived safely. You can elicit pen, paper, stamp, envelop, and post office.
3. Give a student a chance to be the alien, if you would like to extend the activity.

I'm Going on a Picnic

Skills: Listening/Speaking

Time: 5-10 minutes

Age: 8+

Materials: None

This is an oldie, but a goodie. It gets students talking and thinking critically. Think of a rule for items on the picnic, but don't tell the class. For example, "must contain the letter E," or, "must be countable." Tell them you are going on a picnic, and give examples of 3-5 items you are taking with you, to give them hints about your rule. Then, elicit from the students what they would take. If their item doesn't fit your rule, tell them they can't take it.

To keep wait times between turns shorter, have large classes work in groups of 2-3, rather than individually. In any case, set a time limit for each person or group making a guess (30-60 seconds, according to their level), or they are out. The group to guess the rule wins.

Note: groups are not out if they suggest an item that doesn't match the rule, or if they guess the wrong rule. The time limit is to keep the game moving, and disqualifying students for not making guesses keeps students from just listening to other guesses to guess the rule without otherwise contributing.

Procedure:

1. Think of a rule for items which can go on the picnic, such as "must contain the letter E," or, "must be countable."
2. Tell the class you are going on a picnic, and give examples of 3-5 items

you are taking with you, to give them hints about your rule.
3. Elicit from the students what they would take. If their item doesn't fit your rule, tell them they can't take it.
4. Have large classes work in groups of 2-3, and set a 30-60 second time limit to keep wait times between turns shorter.
5. The group to guess the rule wins.

In Front of/Behind/Between

Skills: Listening/Speaking

Time: 5-10 Minutes

Age: 6-10

Materials: Flashcards

Place some flashcards on your board ledge or leaning against the wall at the front of the room. I like to use three sets of three. Place them so that the students can't see the pictures, but show them what is on the flashcards before you place them. Arrange them so that there is one card in front, one in between and one behind. Then, ask some questions such as, "What's in front of the elephant?" or "What's between the giraffe and the gorilla?" The students that can answer the question correctly get a point. I require that students answer the questions in full sentences.

Teaching Tip:

It's easy to adjust the level in this game. To make it easier, reduce the number of flashcards in play. To make it harder, increase the numbers of flashcards and also the variety of questions you ask by including "next to/beside" or "under" and "over/above" if you place some of them in a stack on the table.

Procedure:

1. Place flashcards in three stacks of three on the blackboard ledge or leaning against a wall, so that students can't see the pictures. But, make sure you show the pictures as you are facing them.
2. Choose one student (or a pair) and ask a question. For example, "Where's the elephant?" Students will have to answer, "It's between the monkey and hippo."
3. If correct, the student gets one point.

Last Person Standing

Skills: Speaking/Listening

Time: 5-10 minutes

Age: 6+

Materials: None

Choose a topic based on whatever you're teaching. Some examples are jobs, food, animals, things in the kitchen or classroom, etc. Have all the students stand up in a circle. Clap your hands in a beat 1-2-3 and say a word related to that topic. Continue the 1-2-3 rhythm and have the next person in the circle say a different word related to the topic. If students repeat a word, or don't have one, then they must sit down and the game continues with the remaining players. The game finishes when there is one person standing.

Procedure:

1. Have students stand in a circle and assign a topic.
2. Clap your hands in a 1-2-3 beat and say the first word related to the topic.
3. Continue the rhythm and have the next student say a different word related to the topic. If students repeat a word or don't have one, they must sit down.
4. The game continues until there is one person left standing.

Memory Circle Game

Skills: Speaking/Listening

Time: 5-10 minutes

Age: 7+

Materials: None

This is a game that I often use in classes with a maximum of ten students. To set it up, you need to make a rule about what kind of words or grammar that the students can use. Base it on whatever you are studying that day in class. For example: animals or past tense. You'll need to adjust the rules and criteria according to the level and age of your students. You want to make it challenging, but not impossible so that everyone can have a chance to play at least once in a round. I'll use past tense for my example.

Everyone will stand up, in a circle, and I will start the game off, "I ate pizza." The next student says, "She ate pizza, and I studied English." The next student says, "She ate pizza, he studied English, and I watched TV." And so on it goes, around the circle. If someone forgets someone or gets it incorrect, they are out and have to sit down. I usually let it go until there are 2-3 people left and then I give them a prize of some sort and start over with a new set of criteria.

If you have very low level students, a single word works better. For example, they can say "Cat," "Cat and dog," or "Cat, dog, and fish."

Procedure:

1. Assign a topic or grammar point.
2. All the students stand up in a circle.
3. The first student says a word related to the topic.
4. The next student repeats the first word and adds a new word.
5. The third student repeats the first two words and adds a new one, etc.
6. If students miss a word, they sit down and are out of the game.

Memory Tray

Skills: Speaking

Time: 5-10 minutes

Age: 8+

Materials: A tray with several items/PowerPoint/whiteboard and flashcards

Before class, prepare a tray with 10-20 items, depending on the age of the students. Keep it covered while you tell the students they will have a short time to study the tray. Give 20 seconds to a minute, depending on their age and the number of items. If the class is large, a PowerPoint with images, or flashcards on the whiteboard may be better if you can cover and uncover your whiteboard.

When everyone is ready, uncover the items for the allotted time, and then re-cover them. Have students work in pairs or small groups to reconstruct the tray.

Variation 1: Students simply need to list the items they saw.

Variation 2: Students need to recall the location of the items in relation to one another.

Procedure:

1. In advance, prepare a tray of 10-20 items (more for older students) or a PowerPoint with images or flashcards to put on the whiteboard.
2. Divide the class into pairs or small groups and tell them to look carefully at the items.
3. Tell students not to write anything down.
4. Reveal the items for 20-60 seconds, depending on how many items there are.
5. Have the students work with their partners for 2-3 minutes to reconstruct what they saw.
6. The group with the most correct items wins.

Musical Flashcards

Skills: Speaking

Time: 5 minutes

Age: 6-11

Materials: Flashcards (large enough for the entire class to see), music.

Optional Materials: Timer, second set of flashcards, monitor/overhead projector

Some days, kids are just too antsy to focus especially when the weather is bad and they haven't been able to play at recess. This is good for getting the kids moving around the classroom while still focusing on English.

To set up, have students stand behind their seats with the chair pushed in. Explain to them that as the music plays, they should move in a circle around the class. When the music stops, they stop. You will show them a card. The students must say what it is. If they cannot say it, then they are out and must sit down.

Start the music. Let it play from 5-15 seconds (switch it up each time). Stop the music and quickly show a flashcard. You can go through your deck one at a time and create a discard pile, or you can randomly choose and have some repeats. To make it harder, literally flash the card: show it to the entire class, but for only a few seconds.

Have the students name the flashcard together. If a student doesn't know the word or is too slow to see the flashcard you've shown, then they are out and must sit down.

Variations:

No one gets out, but you need a second set of flashcards. Lay one flashcard on each student desk. Discard any from your deck that are not used. Whoever is in front of that card when you flash it must hold it up and say it. For example, if you hold up a flashcard of an apple, the student standing in front of the desk with the apple flashcard must hold it up and say, "Apple."

For higher-level students, you can have them make a sentence or give the definition, rather than simply say the word.

Teaching Tips:

Unless your class is very small, your students will probably not have a neat circle to move around. So, before you begin, take them on a practice lap or two with you leading the way. To do this, pick a starting point (desk) and have everyone follow you as you move from desk to desk around the entire class. What is important is that they see which direction to move in and where to go when leaving one group of desks or row and joining another.

If you have a large classroom, your set of flashcards should be large enough for the entire class to see. I use A4 flashcards. Another option is to have PowerPoint slides of each card or an overhead projector. If you make your own flashcards, you are probably making them in PPT anyway. If you've made them in portrait, convert them to landscape. There will be a wide border on the left and right, but the image will still be large enough to see.

To keep things moving, I give a 3-finger countdown and have everyone answer together. This game isn't fun indefinitely, so you want to try to cut several students each round.

Procedure:

1. In advance, prepare a set of flashcards and music.
2. To set up, have students stand behind their seat with their chair pushed in.
3. Explain to them that as they music plays, they should move in a circle around the class. When the music stops, they stop. You will show them a card. The students must say what it is. If they cannot say it, they are out and must sit down.
4. Start the music. Let it play from 5-15 seconds (switch it up each time).
5. Stop the music and quickly hold up a flashcard.
6. If a student can't name the flashcard you've shown, they are out and must sit down.
7. Repeat until there is only one student remaining.

Mystery Box

Skills: Speaking

Time: 5-10 minutes

Age: All

Materials: Several small objects, a box

I like to use this activity just after studying adjectives. I'll make sure we have learned words that describe texture as well as the usual size and shape words. This is a fun activity, but it is best with small classes due to the time it takes for each student to have a turn.

Before class, you will need to prepare a large shoe box or similar, by cutting a hole slightly larger than fist-sized and covering the hole. You can use garland or tissue paper, but a handkerchief is fastest and easiest. Whatever you use, the students should not be able to see inside the box, but they should be able to stick their hand inside.

One by one, have students take turns feeling inside the box. As they feel, ask them questions about the size, shape, texture, etc. Once everyone has had a turn, review the answers students gave while feeling and elicit guesses as to what is in the box. As students guess items correctly, pull them from the box. If no one can guess some items, end by showing them to the class.

Due to the time involved with each child feeling inside the box, this activity is best suited to small classes. You can use anything (not sharp), but children's toys are good for this, as well as letter magnets.

Procedure:
1. In advance, prepare a large shoe box or copy paper box by cutting a hand-sized hole and then covering it with a handkerchief, so students can reach in but can't see inside
2. Place several small (not sharp!) objects inside. The class should know the names of the objects.

3. Have students take turns reaching in the box and feeling the objects.
4. As students feel the objects, ask them questions about the size, shape, and texture of the items.
5. When everyone has had a turn, elicit guesses from the students about what they think the objects are.
6. As students correctly identify items, remove them from the box. If the class cannot guess some items, end the activity by showing the remaining items to the class.

Password

Skills: Speaking/Listening

Time: 10-20 minutes

Age: 8+

Materials: List of words, whiteboard

This activity helps students review vocabulary and practice an important skill: describing something they don't know the word for. Divide students into two groups. The groups will alternate sending a team member to stand at the front of the class with his/her back to the board. Write a word over the person's head, so the team mates can see it but the student cannot. The team must give that person hints until he/she guesses the word or time runs out (20-30 seconds). The team with the most points wins.

Variation:

Have one team's turn last until they run out of time (2-4 minutes) and then switch. This gives an advantage for correctly guessing more quickly. Pause the clock between answers so a new team member can take the hot seat.

Procedure:
1. In advance, prepare a list of words. These can be vocabulary taught in class or just words you expect your students to know.
2. Divide class into two groups.
3. Have groups alternate sending a member to the front of the class, or give each group a time limit of 2-4 minutes and rotate team members as soon as one guesses a word, until time is up.
4. Write a word on the whiteboard over that person's head, so his/her team can see it, but the student cannot.
5. That student's team must give the person hints until he/she guesses the word or time runs out (20-30 seconds).
6. The team with the most points at the end of all the rounds is the winner.

Puzzle Finder

Skills: Speaking/Listening

Time: 10-15 minutes

Age: 8+

Materials: Puzzle pieces (from an actual puzzle or a cut and laminated image)

The objects of this activity are both teamwork (to create the puzzle) and a review of common vocabulary, such as colors, shapes, and common objects. Before class, you should either prepare a puzzle with enough pieces for each student to have one or two each, or print an image which you cut into the correct number of pieces and laminate. The former is easier, but the latter gives you much more flexibility and you can cut the pieces as large as you like.

In order for students to put the puzzle together correctly, they will need to be able to describe their piece to others as they mingle looking for adjacent pieces, as well as listen to others' descriptions.

Procedure:
1. In advance, either get a puzzle with enough pieces for each student to have one or two (so, no 500 piece monster puzzles) or print an image (A3 or larger), cut it into the right number of pieces, and laminate it.
2. Give each student a puzzle piece or two, and instruct them to work together to complete the puzzle.
3. According to the level of the students, allow them to show each other the pieces as they work or require them to describe the shape of their piece and the image fragment.

QR Code Hunt

Skills: Speaking/Listening

Time: 15-60 minutes

Age: 8+

Materials: Internet access, printer, tape/Blu-tack, student phones with QR code reader apps installed

This activity requires a bit more prep than others, but (as of writing) the novelty factor is high enough to draw some students in who might otherwise be too cool for school. Classtools.net makes it easy to use make QR codes.

Procedure:

1. In advance, write your questions in a Word document. These can be discussion questions, trivia questions (pub quiz), or you can pre-test student levels, particularly if you are teaching a subject class.
2. Go to http://www.classtools.net/QR/ and copy and paste.
3. Create the QR codes and print.
4. Post the printouts in various places around the class, or better yet, a larger area.
5. Before dividing students into groups, make sure at least one member of each group has a QR code reader on their phone. If not, give them a minute to download an app—there are plenty of them and most older students will already have one.
6. Divide students into groups of 3-4 and give them a time limit to find and answer all of the questions.
7. Particularly if you plan to assess student levels, as an option you can have students write the questions they find, and their answers.
8. Wrap up the class with a group discussion of the answers.

Show and Tell

Skills: Speaking/Listening

Time: 1-2 minutes per student (no questions). 4-6 minutes per student (with questions)

Age: 6+

Materials: None

This is a classic activity from way back in elementary school but it can work well in your ESL classes too. Tell students a few days before the "show and tell" class that they need to bring an object from home that is meaningful to them. If it's something really big (a piano) or something that doesn't transport easily (a cat), then they can email you a picture to put up on the screen instead. Students give a short presentation, talking about the item and why it's meaningful to them. The audience can ask a few follow-up questions. In order to make the question time go more smoothly with shy classes, you can put students into teams of 4-6 and each team has to ask one question. You could also award points or a reward to the 3 or 4 students who ask the most thoughtful questions.

Procedure:

1. Tell students to bring a meaningful object from home, or send a picture if bringing the object isn't practical.

2. Students introduce the object in a short presentation of 1-2 minutes, depending on the level.

3. The other students listen and can ask some follow-up questions.

S-O-S Game

Skills: Speaking/Listening

Time: 10-15 minutes

Age 8+

Materials: whiteboard and a list of questions

I like to play the S-O-S game as a way to review whatever we studied in the previous class. For example, maybe the grammar point was countable/uncountable nouns. It can get quite complicated, so it's something I'd for sure want to review before moving on with new material.

I'm sure you know the game S-O-S from when you were a kid. Draw a 6x6 grid on the board. Give the grid numbers and letters to make it easier for the students to pick what box they want. Then, divide the students up into teams of 4 or 5 and give them each a symbol (triangle, square, star, heart, etc.). Then ask review questions, going from team to team in order. Simple, easy questions with a definite right or wrong answer are best to keep this game moving quickly. A correct answer gets them a square on the board, where you will put their symbol. You can do 6 or 7 rounds, and by this time the good teams will have 2 or 3 points. The top team gets a prize of some kind.

Teaching Tip:

This game gets boring after 15 minutes or so, so don't plan on playing this for an entire class. It works best as a warm-up review game. You can also teach the students the rules and have them play in groups of 4-5, which will make this activity far more student-centered. Give each group a list of review questions that you write up and print out and act as a referee, if necessary.

Procedure:

1. Prepare a list of review questions.

2. Put students into groups of 4-5 to play as a class, or have them play in small groups with each other.

3. Students do rock-scissor-paper and the first student answer the first question. If correct, they mark their symbol on the board. If incorrect, there is no penalty but they don't get to mark the board.

4. The next student answers the next question and follows the same procedure.

5. The goal is to get as many 3-in-a-rows as possible with their symbol.

Steal the Eraser

Skills: Listening/Speaking

Time: 10-15 minutes

Age: 6+

Materials: 2 chairs, a table or desk, eraser

Divide the students into two teams. Have two desks at the front of the class, facing each other with an eraser in the middle of the two desks. One student from each team comes and sits in the hot seat. Rotate through the class so that all the students get a chance to play at least once. You then ask a question of some sort, which you should prepare beforehand (one round = one question/2 students. Two rounds = one question/student. Include a few extras for a "bonus" round). The first person that grabs the eraser can try to answer the question. A helpful rule is that the student can take the eraser whenever they want, but the teacher stops talking as soon as the eraser is touched. The student then has ten seconds to answer as you count down on your fingers. If correct, they get one point. If not, the other player gets a chance to answer the question after you repeat the full question one more time.

To make it even more exciting or if one team is behind by a lot of points, have a "Bonus Round," where the teams pick their best three players and each question is worth three points.

Procedure:
1. Prepare two desks facing each at the front of the class, with an eraser in the middle.
2. Divide students into two teams.
3. Each team sends up one person to the front and they sit at the desks. I don't let students choose the person for each round but simply make them go in the order that they are sitting.
4. The teacher asks a question (prepare the list beforehand), but stops speaking once the eraser is touched. Alternatively, you can have each team appoint a captain who takes turns reading the prepared list of questions in order to increase student talking time.

5. The first player to touch the eraser must answer the question within ten seconds. Count down the time on your fingers.
6. If correct, he/she gets one point and the next two people come up to the front for another question.
7. If incorrect, the teacher reads the question (in full) one more time and the opposing player gets a chance to answer the question within ten seconds.
8. If correct, they get one point. If incorrect, both players sit down and the next pair comes up. You can share the correct answer with the class before saying a new question.
9. Continue until all students have had a chance to play at least once.

Student Engineers

Skills: Speaking/Listening

Time: 5-10 minutes

Age: 6+

Materials: Disposable cups and pipe cleaners/uncooked spaghetti/wooden skewers

Optional Materials: Ticking time bomb sound effect

This is a popular activity and is easy to adjust according to what materials you have on hand or can acquire easily. Divide the class into groups of 3-4 and give each group the same assortment of items. Easy ones to prepare are disposable cups and pipe cleaners/uncooked spaghetti/skewers. Give them a building task, such as building the tallest tower.

Procedure:

1. In advance, prepare "building materials" so each group has the same assortment of items. You want them to have plenty of each item, at least 20-30 cups and skewers, for example.
2. Divide the class into groups of 3-4 students and give each group the same assortment of items.
3. Give them a building task, such as building the tallest tower, and a time limit. The shorter the time, the more pressure will be on, and the more fun to watch.
4. When time is up, the group with the tallest tower is the winner.

Talk Show

Skills: Speaking/Listening

Time: 15 minutes

Age: 6+

Materials: None

Optional Materials: Toy microphones, video clip with monitor

This is a pair work variation of self-introductions. My higher level students tend to find this more fun than the same old self-introductions they do all the time. I set up the front of the class as a talk show set with a desk and chair (for the host) and a chair for the person being interviewed. Then, I divide the students into pairs. Before beginning, I introduce the activity by asking students about talk shows. Most students will be very familiar with the concept. We then discuss what kinds of questions a host might ask.

One pair at a time comes to the front and the two students take turns being the host and the guest. The host is given either a set number of questions to ask or a time limit. After each host's time is up, the teacher can open the floor to "audience" questions.

Teaching Tips:

While introducing the topic, it may be helpful to brainstorm a written list of questions on the whiteboard for them to refer to as needed. However, you will need to remind them that talk show hosts look at the person as they ask questions.

The larger the class, the less time each pair will have to speak in front of the class. So, if your class is very large, limit each pair to 2-3 questions each before switching roles. If you have a large class and a short period, this may not be a feasible activity for even an entire class period.

Procedure:

1. Before class, set up a desk and chair and another chair, similar to the set-up of a talk-show.

2. To demonstrate, show the class a short clip of a popular celebrity being interviewed on a talk show to show the class, or simply talk about talk shows: what kinds of questions are asked, etc.

3. Divide students into pairs: interviewer/host and guest. (They will switch roles.)

4. Have one pair at time come to the front of the class (the audience) and conduct their interviews. The guests are playing themselves—this is a self-introduction.

5. After a set number of questions (about 5) or your time limit, allow questions to be asked by the audience. Then, have the students switch roles.

Telephone

Skills: Listening/speaking

Time: 5-10 minutes

Age: 8+

Materials: None

Everyone has played telephone before. Students are lined up in two or more rows (teams) starting from the front and going to the back. The student at front of each team is given a sentence. You need to consider the level of the students carefully when choosing your sentence—make sure the first students can all understand it really easily. It can work well to take something that you've been studying from the textbook and adjust it slightly. They whisper the sentence one time to the next student. That student whispers it to the person in front of them, etc. The last person to hear the sentence must correctly state what they have heard.

The team with the closest phrase is the winner. You may need to explicitly forbid students from using their L1. This is usually obvious if the ending sentence has the same meaning as the original but uses synonyms.

Teaching Tips:

All teams can have the same sentence or you can give each a different one. I like to take the heads of each team into the hall, give each a different sentence and allow them the chance to have it repeated before we begin. Then, the students return together and the game begins.

Keep the teams to about 8-10 students or fewer in order to increase speaking time. Remember that students will only say one sentence each per round. Remind students that even if they didn't hear the sentence clearly, they need to make their best guess and tell *something* to the next person instead of nothing.

Procedure:

1. Divide students into teams, unless you have a very small class. Larger teams will make for funnier results.
2. Have the teams stand in line, starting from the front to the back.
3. Have the first students from each team join you in the hall. Give each a sentence to repeat and return together when each is satisfied they know

what to say.

4. The students whisper the sentence once to the next person, who whispers it to the next person and so on.

5. The last student in each line says the sentence they heard.

6. The group with the sentence closest to the original wins.

Typhoon

Skills: Listening/Speaking

Time: 20-30 minutes

Age: 6+

Materials: whiteboard and questions

    This is a fun review game that any age group of students will love that requires a little preparation but no materials. Every single time I play it, my students always want to play again and talk about it for the rest of the semester. Draw a grid on the board, marking one row with numbers and one with letters. 5x5 works well for a 30 minute game. Put in two or three of each of the special letters (T/H/V), secretly on your master paper, but not the board. On the board will just be a blank grid.

T = typhoon: lose all your points

H = hurricane: pick 1 team for minus 5 points

V = vacation: get 5 points for free

E = easy question: 1 point

M = medium question: 3 points

D = difficult question: 5 points

Fill in the rest of your grid with these easy, medium and difficult questions. Then depending on how big your class is, make 4-5 teams. They pick a square, (B-6 for example), then you write the letter in the box and ask them the question or reveal the "special square" that corresponds to it. Have a list of easy/medium/hard questions prepared beforehand. If they get the question correct, give them the points and if not, erase the letter in the box and another team can pick that square if they want and get the same question.

Procedure:
1. Prepare review questions beforehand, as well as a "grid" with the appropriate letters marked on it (T, H, V, E, M, D).
2. Write the corresponding grid on the whiteboard, but be sure not to reveal the letters. It should just be blank at this point.
3. Put the students into 4-5 teams. They can rock-scissor-paper to decide who goes first. The first team chooses a square and then you reveal which letter it contains. If a special square, perform that action and if a question, ask the appropriate level of question. If the answer is correct, they get the points and that square is finished. If incorrect, nothing happens and that square remains in the game.
4. The next team chooses a square, performs the action, and so on it goes with the next team.
5. Keep track of the total points and continue until all squares are revealed.

Used Card Salesman

Skills: Speaking/Listening

Time: 15-20 minutes

Age: 8+

Materials: Playing cards cut into pieces

This is a negotiation activity. In advance, take a deck of playing cards and cut each card into an equal number of pieces (2-4; the more pieces, the longer the game). Mix the cut cards and divide into the number of groups you will have.

Divide the class into groups of 3-5 and give each group their pile of cards. Give them 2-3 minutes to sort their cards and see how many complete cards they can make with the pieces that they have, and which pieces they need to complete their cards. Once the cards have been sorted, instruct them to complete their missing sets. Give them a time limit of about 10 minutes.

The goal is to have the largest number of completed cards at the end. Students will have to negotiate with other groups, trying to get missing pieces while trying to keep all of the pieces they have. You will soon see which group has the slickest salesmen.

Procedure:
1. Prepare a deck of playing cards by cutting each card into 2-4 pieces.
2. In class, tell the students that they must practice their salesmanship on their classmates. Explain that they will receive cut up cards and must try to make sets of complete cards. At the end of the activity, the group with the most sets will win.

3. Divide the class into groups of 3-5 and give each group an equal share of the mixed card pieces.
4. Allow 2-3 minutes to sort the cards, so each group can see which card pieces they have and make note of which pieces they need to complete a set (a set being a complete card).
5. Give students ten minutes to complete their missing sets, but don't give them any further rules. They should consider as a group whether it would be better to work together or split up and approach different groups at once.
6. When time is up, have each group tally how many complete sets they have and how many single card pieces they still have.

Vocabulary Apples to Apples

Skills: Listening/Speaking

Time: 30+ minutes, including deck-building

Age: 8+

Materials: Paper, pen/pencils, textbooks, scissors

Apples to Apples is a game in which players defend their choice of card played. This version is somewhat different than the actual Apples to Apples game, in order to increase speaking time. Before playing, students need to make two decks of cards using vocabulary words. This is best done at the end of a semester or book, so that there are more words to play with. You may also want to encourage them to brainstorm words they've learned previously.

For deck-building, divide the students into at least two groups: nouns and adjectives. If you have a large class, you may want to further divide them, for example, into person, place and thing groups. The groups should compile as many nouns and adjectives as they can. To keep the two decks easily identifiable, you can use two colors of paper or blank and ruled paper that has been cut into 8-10 pieces.

Collect the cards once the groups have finished creating them and keep the nouns and adjectives separate. Divide the class into groups of 5-8 students and have each group pick a judge. This person will be in charge of the decks of cards and also will have to choose the winner of each round. Each judge should be given an equal share of the two decks.

Have one group help you play a demonstration round in which you are the judge. Deal each group member five noun cards. Turn over one adjective card and have each student choose the noun card in his/her hand that best matches the adjective and give it to you. Read each of their cards and have students explain why their word is the best match. When all students have spoken, announce which card is the winner, and why.

Have the judge in each group deal five noun cards to their groups and turn over/display one adjective card per round. Players must choose the noun card in his/her hand that they feel best matches that adjective and give it to the judge. The judge takes all of the noun cards and shows each card one at a time. Players must defend their card when the judge shows it.

Example:

If the judge draws the word "*big*," the other students may submit nouns like "*watermelon*," "*elephant*," "*heart*," and "*day*." The students can then defend their choices with a single sentence:

A: A watermelon is a big fruit.

B: An elephant is a big animal.

C: A kind person has a big heart.

D: An important day is a big one.

The students should then be encouraged to keep talking in order to convince the judge that their answer is the best.

When all players have spoken, the judge will decide the winner of that round. Each player will be given one more noun card by the judge. The judge will then give both decks to the winner of the round and that person becomes the new judge. He/she turns over the next adjective card to start the next round. If there are not many cards (vocabulary words) to play with, you may want to mix the discards back in to the live decks.

Procedure:

1. Before class, prepare cards by cutting sheets of colored printer paper into 8-10 pieces. Use two different colors.

2. Divide students into groups to build two decks of cards: nouns and adjectives. Students should use their textbooks and also brainstorm as many words as they can and write one word per card.

3. When the decks are ready, divide the students into groups of 5-8.\

4. Divide the two decks equally between the groups and keep the two separate.

5. Have one group come to the front of the class to demonstrate. You will be the judge.

6. Turn over one adjective card. Have your group look at their cards, choose the noun that best matches the adjective, and give it to you.

7. Read each noun card and have the student who gave it to you defend his/her choice (see example above). Choose the best answer and tell the class why.

8. Have groups play rock-scissors-paper to choose the first judge for their group and play one round.

9. After each round, each player is dealt a new noun card, and the winner becomes the new judge (or you can have them rotate in a circle.)

10. Used cards can be mixed back into the decks if there aren't many cards.

"What Can I do with a _____?"

Skills: Speaking/Listening

Time: 5-10 minutes

Age: All

Materials: An object

Show students some random common object (potatoes are often used for this activity, but I like to use some kind of "trash" to introduce a lesson on recycling.) Have students work as a class or in small groups to brainstorm as many possible uses for the item as possible. Give them a time limit (3-5 minutes), then discuss their answers. If some answers seem too outlandish, have the student or group explain how or why they would use the item in that way.

Procedure:
1. Prepare an object. A potato is commonly used, but it can be anything.
2. Divide students into groups of 3-5.
3. Give them 3-5 minutes to brainstorm creative uses for the object.
4. As a class, briefly discuss their various ideas.
5. You can have the class choose the best idea, if you like.

Where Are They Now?

Skills: Speaking/Writing

Time: 10-15 minutes

Age: 8+

Materials: None

This is a post-reading extension activity that can be done orally or in writing. When you finish a novel or story, have the student imagine the main character five or ten years in the future. Where are they? What are they doing? How have the events in the story affected his/her life?

Teaching Tip:

If your student has difficulty, help them with brainstorming. Show him/her how to make a mind map with items such as: relationship, job, hobbies, home, pet, etc. Talk with your student about how his or her own life has changed in the past five or ten years.

Procedure:

1. After reading a story or novel, discuss how the character changed over the course of the story and why.
2. Have your student write or discuss what he/she thinks the character's life is like five or ten years in the future.

Would You Rather

Skills: Speaking/Listening

Time: 5-10 minutes

Age: 6+

Materials: List of questions

"Would You Rather?" is a fun party game. You can buy ready-made decks, but they aren't ESL specific. I make my own cards, but you can just make a list of questions or do this without materials if you can think of choices on the spot. One example is "Would you rather have eyes like a fly, or eyes like a spider?"

The student must choose one and explain why. You can also share your answer and have a short discussion about it.

Procedure:

1. In advance, prepare cards with two choices—the weirder, the better. For example: "Would you rather have eyes like a fly, or eyes like a spider?" If you want to do this without cards, simply give the student two choices.

2. Have a 1-2 minute discussion. The student can also ask you a question if they would like.

You're an Artist!

Skills: Listening

Time: 5-10 minutes

Age: 7-11

Materials: whiteboard, markers

This is a fun way for children to show off their artistic skills while reviewing some vocabulary at the same time. Kids (and adults) love writing on the whiteboard so students seem to really enjoy this activity. It's best played with small classes of fewer than eight students so that everyone can draw at the same time, but if you have a large class you can make it into a team competition. Have the students arrange themselves behind the student at the board in lines and play enough rounds so that everyone is able to draw at least once.

The way it works is that each student has a box on the whiteboard with his/her name above it (or team name). You call out a word, either simple nouns like "banana" or "dog," or phrases like, "A man is running" or "The student is studying." Give the students a set amount of time (1-2 minutes) to draw their picture and then you can judge their artwork and declare the winner of that round.

Procedure:

1. Have students line up at the board. Each student has a square to draw in with his/her name at the top and a marker.

2. Call out a word or phrase and the students have to draw it in a certain amount of time (1-2 minutes).

3. Judge who has the best picture at the end of the round.

Reading

Concentration

Skills: Reading

Time: 10-15 minutes

Age: 6+

Materials: Concentration cards

This is a memory game designed to help students remember vocabulary words and definitions. Make up sets of cards with words on half the cards and the matching definition on the other half. A total of 16 cards (8 sets of words and definitions) works well. Make enough cards so that there is one set for each group of four students.

Students mix up the cards and put them face-down on the desk in an organized fashion. The students play rocks-scissors-paper. The first student chooses two cards and places them face up on the desk so that everyone is able to see them. If they make a set, the student keeps the cards (they're removed from the game), gets one point and is able to choose again. If they don't make a set, the student places them face-down in the **same spot** (it's a memory game!) and the game continues with the next student.

Procedure:
1. Make concentration card sets of words and definitions (16 cards per set, one set per four students).
2. Have students mix the cards and place them face down on the desk in an

organized manner.

3. The first student chooses two cards and places them face up on the desk. If they make a set, the student keeps the cards and get one point. If they don't make a set, the student places them face down in the same spot and the game continues with the next student who reveals two more cards.
4. The winner is the student with the most points.

Correction Relay

Skill: Reading/Writing

Time: 10+ minutes

Age: 8+

Materials: Worksheet

    This is an activity that uses speed and competition to make something old (error correction) new again. Students of all levels should be quite familiar with finding and correcting errors in sentences. By adding a relay aspect, it will (hopefully) make an important but sometimes tedious skill new and more interesting.

    To prepare the activity, create a worksheet with 10-15 errors. You can focus your errors on one aspect of vocabulary, such as synonyms and antonyms, or more simply, misuse vocabulary words in sentences. For lower level students, limit the errors to one per sentence. Higher levels can handle multiple errors in one sentence, and you can increase the challenge by having one vocabulary error per sentence and one or more other errors, such as grammar or punctuation mistakes.

The activity itself is straightforward. Students will work in teams of 4-5 to correct the worksheet as quickly as possible. Each student makes one correction and passes the worksheet to the next person who makes the next correction. They continue to pass the worksheet around until it is complete. You can make it easier by allowing students to choose any remaining sentence to correct, or you can require them to work from top to bottom.

Procedure:
1. In advance, prepare a worksheet with 10-15 sentences containing vocabulary errors.
2. Divide students into groups of 4-5. If possible, group the desks to facilitate easy passing of the worksheets.
3. Have students take turns making one correction and, passing the worksheet to the next student to make one correction. They continue passing and correcting until the worksheet is complete.
4. When all teams are finished, go over the errors as a class. The team with the most correct sentences wins.

Disappearing Words

Skills: Reading

Time: 10 minutes

Age: 6+

Materials: whiteboard

This vocabulary game is an easy way to get students to keep a set of new vocabulary words in their heads, or to review past words. Write down 10-15 words on the whiteboard and give students 1-2 minutes to study them. Then, if you have a big class, ask everyone to close their eyes as you choose one or two words to erase. Students open their eyes and have to tell you what is missing and where it was. If you have a small class, you can choose individual students to close their eyes and then tell you the missing word(s) after you've erased them. You can either write those words in their spots again or add new words to the mix and continue the game.

Procedure:

1. Write down 10-15 vocabulary words on the whiteboard.
2. Have student(s) close their eyes as you erase 1-2 words.
3. Students open their eyes and tell you which words are missing and where they were.
4. You can write those same words back in, or add new words to the mix in those same spots and continue the game.

Extensive Reading Context Clues

Skill: Reading

Time: 10+ minutes

Age: 10+

Materials: Story or novel

This activity helps students develop their ability to use context clues when reading. Simply have them write down five words they do not know as they are reading. Have them note the page number and paragraph to easy reference. Once they have finished reading, have them find those words again and write down the sentence it is used in as well as the sentence before and after it.

Once they have written these sentences, have them use the sentences to guess the meaning of each unknown word and write that as well. Finally, have them compare their guess to the dictionary definition. Are they close? If not, was the word used in an ambiguous way, or could they have made better use of context clues?

Procedure:

1. As an addition to a regular reading activity, have your students make note of five words in the story they do not know.

2. Have them make note of each word, the page number, and the paragraph number and continue reading.

3. Once they have finished reading, have them go back and find those words again and write down the sentence it is used in as well as the sentence before and after it.

4. Then, have them use the sentences to guess the meaning of each unknown word and write that as well.

Flyswatter

Skills: Listening/Reading

Time: 5-10 minutes

Age: 7+

Materials: whiteboard, 2 flyswatters

This is a game that can really energize your class at the end of a long day or semester. It makes an excellent way to review any new vocabulary that you've taught or as a warm-up at the beginning of the next class. Write the target words on the board in a random fashion. You can use 10-20 depending on the age and level of students. Divide the students into two teams. One person from each team comes up to the whiteboard and each person is given a flyswatter. Give hints to describe one of the words and the first student to hit the word with the flyswatter gets a point for his/her team. If two students go for a word at the same time, the one on the bottom of the flyswatter stack gets the point. If a student makes an incorrect choice, he/she is out (no second chances). I usually start with a very general hint and progress to more specific ones where the answer is quite obvious. It's up to the student whether or not he/she wants to risk it and guess before the answer is apparent to everyone.

Procedure:

1. Divide students into two teams.
2. Write 10-20 vocabulary words on the whiteboard in random fashion.
3. The first two students come to the board and are each given a flyswatter.

4. The teacher gives hints for one of the words, starting with general ones and getting more specific.

5. The student hits the word with his/her flyswatter when he/she knows the answer.

6. If correct, his/her team gets a point and the next two students come to the board. If incorrect, the other student is given a chance to guess the word and the teacher can give more hints if necessary. If both students are incorrect, both will sit down and neither team gets a point.

Find the Reference

Skills: Reading

Time: 10+ minutes

Age: 8+

Materials: Newspaper article, pen

This is a noticing activity. In newspaper writing, care is taken to avoid repetitive use of the subject's name. This is the opposite of most ESL material, which makes frequent use of repetition to reinforce language. Students read a newspaper article and circle all references to the subject in order to practice recognizing the subject even when various terms are used to reference it. For a completed example of this activity, please see: www.eslspeaking.org/reference.

Procedure:

1. Choose an article from a newspaper that has multiple references to the subject but uses a number of different referents such as, "Jones," "he,"

"him," "the 39-year-old," "the painter," "the father of two," etc.

2. Have the students read and circle each reference to the subject.

Stack Attack

Skills: Reading/Speaking

Time: 5+ minutes

Age: 6-11

Materials: Flashcards (one set per pair), small cups (same number as flash cards, plus three or four for a tower base), timer

This is a speed activity. Each round is 30-60 seconds (have longer rounds for more words, or shorter for fewer). In this activity, students work in pairs: one student shows the second student a flashcard and the second student names it. With each word, they should add one cup to their tower. If either of the following happens, the student must start over (both the tower and the stack of flash cards):

1. Students do not say the word correctly or do not know the word (his/her partner should give them the correct answer, so that they can do it the next time.)
2. Their tower falls over.

When the timer goes off, the two students switch roles. The student in each pair whose tower was the tallest wins. You can extend the game with knockout rounds until there is one winner for the class, or you can have students play again with the same partner or a new one.

Variation:

Higher level students can make a sentence or give the definition, rather than (or in addition to) saying the word. Give them enough flashcards for a 90-120 second round.

Teaching Tips:

This one is good for younger kids, but your 9-11 year olds may like it as well. I use the little cups used for dispensing medicine. Sleeves of disposable coffee cups from the school office can work well too. The younger the students, the larger the cup you may want to use. I've also used empty toilet rolls for this, which adds a bit of challenge because they are harder to balance.

Procedure:

1. In advance, prepare one set of flashcards per pair of students, plus a stack of small cups of 3-4 more than the number of flashcards.
2. Have students create a tower base with the extra 3-4 cups by setting them upside down side by side.
3. Set the timer for 30-60 seconds.
4. Have the students work in pairs, with one showing the flashcards one at a time and the other reading it and then stacking one cup on their tower.
5. Students must start over if they do not know the word or if their tower falls.
6. If a student doesn't know a word, their partner should tell them before they start over.
7. When the timer goes off, the pair switches roles.

Story Timeline

Skills: Reading/Listening/Speaking

Time: 10-15 minutes

Age: 6+

Materials: None

Optional Materials: Sentence strips of important events in a novel

Extensive reading is an excellent way to build your students' vocabulary quickly, but you and your students probably don't want to spend too much class time reading novels. What you can do is assign a novel for homework and in each lesson, go over unfamiliar vocabulary or situations as well as any number of extension activities. This is one such activity and it can be done individually or in small groups.

A timeline, or chronology, of important plot events is a useful way to have the class briefly summarize the story chapter by chapter. A timeline will help them keep track of the story while providing practice determining important events. With lower-level students, you may want to scaffold the activity by providing the sentences for the students to order.

Procedure:

1. (Optional) In advance, prepare sentence strips describing important events in the plot.
2. Have the students either order the sentence strips you have provided or determine the events on their own. If you are not using sentence strips, you can have the class complete the activity orally or in writing.

Vocabulary Word Hunt

Skills: Reading/Writing

Time: 5-10 minutes

Age: 8+

Materials: Worksheet

Make a 3 x 3 grid with clues about nine vocabulary words and include a word bank. Have students use their dictionaries or glossaries to race to get 1/2/3 Bingos or complete the grid. Here's an example of vocabulary word hunt: www.eslspeaking.org/vocabulary-word-hunt.

Procedure:

1. Prepare 3 x 3 grids filled with clues about nine vocabulary words and a word bank.
2. Have students use their dictionaries or glossaries to get 1/2/3 Bingos or complete the grid.
3. The first student to correctly match the words with the definitions wins.

Word-Definition Match

Skills: Reading

Time: 5-10 minutes

Age: 7+

Materials: Cards or worksheet/whiteboard/PowerPoint

Card Version: Print one word or definition per card. You will need one set per student, pair or group. This version is good for pair/small group work and adds a speaking component to the task.

Worksheet/whiteboard/PowerPoint Version: Create a word bank of current or review vocabulary and a list of definitions for students to draw a line (worksheet version) or matching letters and numbers for whiteboard or PowerPoint.

Procedure (Card Version):
1. In advance, prepare cards with one word or definition per card. Print and laminate enough for each student, pair or group to have a set.
2. If you're having students work in pairs or small groups, divide the class accordingly and distribute a full set of cards to each. If students will be working alone, give each student a set of cards.
3. Have students match the words to their definitions as quickly as possible.

Procedure (Worksheet/whiteboard/PowerPoint Version):
1. Have students match the words and definitions, by drawing a line (worksheet) or matching letters and numbers and writing their answers in their notebooks.
2. Have students trade papers to check.

Writing

Chapter Response

Skills: Speaking/Writing

Time: 10-15 minutes

Age: 7+

Materials: None

Optional Materials: Printed list of questions

Chapter endings make handy stopping points to check your students' comprehension and build a bit of interest to keep up motivation for the next chapter. These questions can be answered orally as part of a book discussion or written in a reader response journal and then discussed in class.

Some questions you can ask include:

What surprised you in this chapter?

What feelings did you have as you read? What made you feel this way?

What words, phrases, or situations in the chapter would like to have explained to you?

Would you recommend this novel to someone else? Why or why not?

How do the events in this story so far relate to your life?

Which character do you most relate to? In what way?

Which character most reminds you of someone in your life? In what way?

What do you hope to learn about (a character) as you continue reading?

What do you think will happen next?

Procedure:

1. Prepare a printed list of questions about the chapter.
2. Discuss together in class, or have the students write their answers for homework and you can discuss them in the next class.

Character Problems and Solutions

Skills: Speaking/Writing

Time: 10-15 minutes

Age: 7+

Materials: None

    This is a post-reading activity to include in a novel study or use with a short story. Choose a problem a character faced in the story. Discuss the problem and how the character solved it. Then, have your students brainstorm other ways the problem could have been dealt with. This is a sneaky grammar lesson. You can teach modals of regret (could/should/would have done, etc.) without getting too personal with your students..

Procedure:

1. Choose a problem a character faced in the story.

2. Discuss the problem and how the character solved it.

3. Have students brainstorm other ways to deal with the problem.

Choose Your Own Adventure Group Writing

Skills: Speaking/Writing

Time: 1+ class periods

Age: 10+

Materials: Blank story maps

Optional Materials: Story starters

Choose Your Own Adventure stories are fun to read, and can be fun to write. The group aspect can be helpful for brainstorming story ideas and, of course, many hands make light work. Even the students most resistant to writing will appreciate that ¼ of a story is less work than an entire story. *This activity will work best with Intermediate and above students, but adventurous high-beginners could enjoy creating simple stories.

If your students are unfamiliar with this style of story, you can show them this example: www.halfbakedsoftware.com/quandary/version_2/examples/castaway.htm. If you show this example to students above the high-beginner level, make your expectations clear or you may well end up with just a sentence or two from each student.

To begin the writing activity, divide the class into groups of 4. Either give your students a scenario which requires a choice to be made, or allow them to brainstorm their story from start to finish. Each student will need a blank story map to plan their writing. Each group should work together to begin their story, then break into pairs to write the second stage, and finally each write one ending. They will need to discuss the options they write about, so they will each have something different.

Some examples of scenarios are:

A. Your friend falls and breaks a leg while the two of you are hiking. You cannot get a phone signal. Your friend knows how to read a compass and map, but you do not. Do you turn back alone and try to retrace your steps, stay and hope that someone else passes by, or try to carry your friend back?

B. You are on a space ship that has just arrived on a new planet. You don't know what to expect when you open the doors. Do you send one person out to explore alone or stay together? Do you walk out with your weapons ready to fire or with your arms open to show you aren't dangerous?

Each group would need to choose two of the options and break into pairs. Each pair would write about one option and lead to another choice. Since the two pairs are following different options already, they do not need to face the same type of choice, unless you want them to.

When each pair has a new choice to make, each person will choose one option. Working individually, each person will finish the story by following the chosen option. There will be 1 beginning, 2 middles, and 4 endings.

Procedure:

1. Begin by asking your students if they are familiar with Choose Your Own Adventure stories. If not, show the example linked above.
2. Divide students into groups of four. Either give them a scenario (several are suggested above), or have each group brainstorm their own.
3. All four group members will collaborate on the beginning of the story, up to the first point of making a decision.
4. The group will divide into pairs and each pair will collaborate on one option each.
5. When the next option is given, each student will choose one option and write that ending for the story. So, there will be one beginning, two middles, and four endings.

Make a Sentence

Skill: Writing

Time: 5 minutes

Age: 6+

Materials: None, or worksheet/whiteboard/PowerPoint

To practice current or review vocabulary, have students make 1-5 sentences.

No Materials Version: Have students use their books and choose a given number of words to make sentences.

whiteboard/PowerPoint Version: Give students a list of words to use all or some of.

Worksheet/PowerPoint Version: Fill-in-the-blank or multiple choice with a word bank.

Procedure:

Begin with a brief oral review of the vocabulary words you want them to work with and elicit from the students what the words mean.

No Prep Version: Have students take out their books and notebooks and tell them a number of sentences to make using those words. For example, "Turn to page 53, and choose three vocabulary words. In your notebook, write a new sentence using each word."

Whiteboard/PowerPoint Version: Either give students a word list to choose from, or for lower level classes, several sentences with a word bank. Have the students write the complete sentences in their notebooks.

Name 5 Things

Skills: Listening/Writing

Time: 5 minutes

Age: 6+

Materials: Paper, pencil

This is an excellent warm-up activity at the beginning of class to review vocabulary words from the previous class. Put students into pairs. They'll need one piece of paper and one pen. Tell them to name five _____. The category will depend on the level and age of students. For beginners, you could do easy things like animals, colors, fruits, etc. For higher-level students, you could use things that move, animals with four legs, things that can fly, breakfast foods, etc. The first team to write down their five things raises their hands and you can check to make sure all the answers are appropriate.

Procedure:

1. Put students into pairs with one piece of paper and one pencil.
2. Tell the class to, "Name five _____." Each team has to write down five words on their paper.
3. Once a team is finished, they raise their hands.
4. Check to make sure all the team's answers are appropriate.

Proofreading/Editing

Skills: Writing

Time: 5-10 minutes

Age: 8+

Materials: Worksheet/white-board

To keep proper grammar usage fresh in your students' minds, they should practice frequently. This doesn't need to be a full grammar lesson; a quick warm-up activity can do the trick. You can give your students a variety of errors to correct: word choice, word order, punctuation, capitalization, etc. They should write the sentences or passage correctly.

Procedure:

1. In advance, prepare a worksheet. You could even take a previous workbook activity and reproduce it.
2. The sentences or passage should practice previously studied points of grammar by having errors of that sort: word choice, word order, punctuation, capitalization, etc.
3. Have the students correct the errors.

Puzzles

Skills: Reading/Writing

Time: 10-20 minutes

Age: 6+

Materials: A puzzle

Puzzles are an excellent way to review vocabulary and I find that most students enjoy doing them, particularly teenagers. They can also work very well for "quiet" classes that don't have a lot of outgoing students in them where it's hard to do some of the more active games like charades. It's really easy to make puzzles yourself using something like Discovery.com's Puzzlemaker (www.discoveryeducation.com/free-puzzlemaker) and it's actually the preferable option since you can include all the specific vocabulary that you'd like. I prefer to use the criss-cross option because it has the most educational benefit since it deals with meanings as well as vocabulary words.

Procedure:

1. Go to Discovery.com and find the puzzlemaker.
2. Design your puzzle (criss-cross is best!), using words and definitions. Alternatively, you could give hints about the word related to the context you'd use it in instead of the actual definition.
3. Have students complete the puzzle. I usually make it a bit competitive by putting them in pairs and awarding the first couple of teams a prize of some sort.
4. It's up to you whether or not to allow dictionaries or textbooks. In my experience, dictionaries don't really help that much while the course book where the words came from really does. You could also say that for the first five minutes, they must only use their brains, but they can use anything they want after that. If there is a particularly hard one that no student is able to get, I'll give the entire class a hint.

Q & A

Skills: Writing
Time: 10 minutes
Age: All
Materials: None
Optional Materials: Worksheet/whiteboard/PowerPoint

In this activity, students will use one vocabulary word to make a question and another to answer the question.

No materials version: Students will use their vocabulary list/text book to choose their two words.

Worksheet/whiteboard/PowerPoint version: Give your students a word list to work from. This is good if you want to review specific terms, or if you want students to focus on specific terms from their current vocabulary list.

Procedure:
1. In advance, prepare a worksheet or PowerPoint with a word bank of vocabulary words. Otherwise, write a word list on the whiteboard or tell your students which page in their text book you want them to work from.
2. Have students write two sentences in their notebooks: one should ask a question using a vocabulary word and the other should answer the question using a different vocabulary word.
3. Give students a time limit of 3-5 minutes.

Scaffolded Writing Prompts

Skill: Writing

Time: 10+ minutes

Age: 6+

Materials: Scaffolded prompts

You may often be required to have students write beyond their actual level. The fastest way to get them from where they are to where you are required to take them is to provide scaffolded writing prompts. The level of scaffolding will depend on their level and the level of writing expected.

For your lowest-level students, this will look a lot like MadLibs. You will provide the bulk of the text, and they will make additions from choices you also provide. Toward the other end of the spectrum, you can provide example test essays with connectors and hedges removed, so they can practice using those correctly. For a greater challenge, you could provide the first sentence of each paragraph in an essay, and have the students complete the essay.

A basic high-beginner scaffolded writing activity I do is give students a journal prompt with a mind map which I have started for them. Depending on the prompt, I will create several lists on the mind map and fill in at least one example on each list. I may also include a list of useful words related to the topic. Students begin by filling in their mind map, then write their journal. This helps them think through what they want to say and helps them create a cohesive, understandable journal entry.

Procedure:

1. In advance, create a scaffolded writing prompt for your students. Depending on their level, this may include useful vocabulary, a mind map or similar pre-writing task, and/or a partially written text.
2. Have students begin by filling in any pre-writing task, then complete the main writing activity.

Scoot

Skills: Reading/Writing

Time: 20+ minutes

Age: 7-11

Materials: Flashcards (you will need to number them) or task cards, timer, answer sheets

If you haven't played Scoot before, it's a fun way to get kids moving. Because there is a time limit and they are moving, they don't feel like the exercises are such a chore. If you haven't used task cards before, they are flashcard-sized cards with one "task" on each one. The task can be whatever you want them to practice, everything from unscrambling vocabulary words to alphabetizing to sentence correction and so on.

To play, lay one card face down on each desk. Give students an answer sheet or have them use their notebooks. When you start the timer, they turn over the cards and record their answers. When timer rings, they turn the card back over and move to the next seat. Repeat until they have gone around the room and are back in their own seats.

The age and the level of the students will affect what type of tasks you can use for Scoot. For lower-level students, use multiple choice activities, such as choosing the correct spelling of a vocabulary word (with or without a picture), alphabetical order of three words or syllable division. For advanced students, the task may be to write the definition of a given word or an original sentence.

Procedure:

1. In advance, prepare a set of flashcards or task cards and a timer. You may also want to prepare answer sheets, or you can have students use their notebooks.
2. To begin, lay one card face down on each desk.
3. Give students an answer sheet or have them use their notebooks.
4. When you start the timer, they turn over the card and record their answer.
5. When timer rings, they turn the card back over and move to the next seat.
6. Repeat until they have gone around the room and are back in their own seats.
7. You can check answers together if there is only one correct answer possible, or you can collect them.

Scrabble

Skill: Writing

Time: 10-15 minutes

Age: 7+

Materials: Oversized wall-mounted board, or one board per table and a set of letters

Your students will likely be familiar with Scrabble, either the board game or similar apps. It's a great way to get students to recall vocabulary and use correct spelling. It's a bit labor intensive to create the board(s), but I get several years of use out of a wall-mounted board.

To make a wall-mounted board, I use a large (big enough for letters to be seen across the classroom) piece of felt. Thin quilt batting is not as durable, but may be easier to come by. The Velcro on the back of the letters will pull bits of it off, but I still can get enough use out of a board to make it a viable option. I use an actual board as a guide for number of squares and arrangement of "special" squares, but I add in a few more than in the standard game. Wikipedia has the official list of number of letters and point value, which I use as well.

I make the letter cards about the size of my hand so that the words can be read across the classroom. I laminate them (of course!) and stick a square of "pointy" Velcro on the back. Since the board is felt or batting, the Velcro sticks right on.

If the class is lower-level, I have the students work in pairs or threes. If the class is quite large, I use table-top game boards. You can splurge and pay for real boards, but I just use A3 paper. I make a top board and bottom board, print them, cut off the border at the join, laminate them, and tape them together. You will need a set of letters of the appropriate size, but you don't need Velcro.

Procedure:
1. In advance, prepare one wall-mounted board with letter cards with Velcro on the back, or enough game boards and letter sets for each table to have one. (I use Wikipedia for the game board layout and letter point values and numbers.)
2. Depending on class size and level, have students work as individuals, pairs, or threes. (A large class playing as individuals on a wall-mounted board will create a lot of downtime.)

Synonym/Antonym Brainstorm Race

Skill: Writing

Time: 5 minutes

Age: 8+

Materials: Large paper (one piece per group) or whiteboard and markers (at least one per group)

This is activity to be used with new vocabulary, after introducing the terms and definitions. To play, divide students into groups of 4-5 and give each group at least one marker. If you are not using the whiteboard, also give each group one piece of A3 or butcher paper. Give students a time limit of 2-3 minutes to list all of the vocabulary words they can remember from the previous lesson. With higher-level classes, have students add a synonym, antonym, or brief definition. The group with the most correct words wins.

Procedure:

1. In advance, prepare markers and optionally, a piece of A3 or butcher paper for each group.
2. Divide students into groups of 4-5.
3. Have students work together to list all of the vocabulary and add at least one synonym and antonym of each word.
4. The group with the most correct words wins.

Vocabulary Square

Skill: Writing

Time: 20+ minutes

Age: 10+

Materials: Index cards (students should be told in advance to bring one card per vocabulary word); dictionary or textbook with glossary

This is a class activity to facilitate self-study as well as dictionary skills. Many students these days rely on their electronic dictionaries for translations and don't develop their English- English dictionary skills. They may also not realize the benefits of flashcards for vocabulary self-study. Regular repetition of exposure to new words is necessary to commit them to working memory.

It is an easy activity to set up. Have students divide their index into four corners:

1. Write the meaning in the students' own words.
2. Write at least one synonym and one antonym.
3. Write an example sentence.
4. Draw an image representing the term.

Remind students to review the flashcards at least once a day.

Procedure:

1. At least one class in advance, ask students to bring index cards. Alternatively, you can cut copy paper into 8 pieces, but it is not as durable.
2. Explain to students that flashcards are a great way to learn new vocabulary if they review the cards often.

3. Have students divide their index cards into four corners, and fill as follows:

- Write the meaning in the students' own words.
- Write at least one synonym and one antonym.
- Write an example sentence.
- Draw an image representing the term.

Word of the Day

Skills: Writing

Time: 5 minutes

Age: 6+

Materials: whiteboard/PowerPoint

I have frequently been required to either give my students a word, quote, or idiom of the day, outside of our usual text, but it's usually related to the text or a monthly theme. You can easily start a Word of the Day activity for your students, by giving them a single word each day from their text (but not a vocabulary word), current events or by having a theme for each month.

Write the word on the whiteboard or PowerPoint along with the definition, part of speech, and several example sentences. Have students copy all of this in their notebooks in a section for their Words of the Day. You can use the word as an exit ticket, have a weekly quiz, or add one or two words to each regular vocabulary quiz.

Variation (more advanced): Idiom of the Day is where you give students an idiom with a definition and a picture (if possible). Have them make 1-3 sentences using it correctly.

Procedure:

1. In advance, prepare a collection of words from your students' textbook but not part of the vocabulary list.
2. Begin each day (or one day per week) with one new word. Introduce the word just as you would their regular vocabulary: present the word, the definition, part of speech and several example sentences.
3. Have students copy the sentences in the notebooks and add their own sentence.
4. Add all or some Words of the Day to your regular vocabulary quizzes.

Word Poem / Name Poem

Skills: Writing

Time: 10-20 minutes

Age: 8+

Materials: Example poem poster/PowerPoint

Another activity you undoubtedly did yourself as a student. Either give students a word related to the lesson, or have them use their names (a great ice breaker activity, too!) They simply begin each line with a letter from the word, so that the first letter of each line read vertically spells the word. Using that letter, write a word or phrase that describes the word.

Here's an example word poem: www.eslspeaking.org/word-poem.

Teaching Tip:

These are great for decorating the classroom or including in student portfolios.

So, have them make a final draft on copy paper and decorate. The final draft can be done as homework.

Procedure:
1. In advance, prepare your own name or word poem to display for students.
2. Show them that the first letter of each line spells a word.
3. Give them a word related to your lesson or have them use their names to make their own poem.

Icebreaker/Warm-Up

2 Truths and a Lie

Skills: Writing/Reading/Listening/Speaking

Time: 20-30 minutes

Age: 10+

Materials: None

Play in groups of 4-6 in a bigger class, or everyone together in a small class. My general rule is that if you allow minimal or no follow-up questions, it takes around 3-4 minutes per student. However, if you allow 2-3 minutes of questions, it takes about 6-7 minutes per student. It's a good activity to use "always, usually, sometimes, never" or "can, can't" and "I've." Students write three sentences, one of which is false. They read their sentences and the other students guess the false one. Higher level classes can ask three questions, or question the person for a pre-determined amount of time (2-3 minutes) to determine the false one. A correct guess gets one point. Each student gets a turn to play.

Procedure:
1. Write three sentences on the board about yourself: two are true and one is not.
2. Explain to students that they are to do the same for themselves.
3. Do your demonstration with one group. Read your sentences and those students can ask three questions.

4. Each student in the group must choose for themselves which sentence is false. Reveal the answer and whoever guessed correctly gets a point.
5. The students play the game in small groups, making sure that each person gets a chance to share their three statements. You can help move the activity along by acting as a time-keeper by giving each student's turn a specific time limit.

Alphabet Game

Skills: Writing

Time: 5 minutes

Age: 6+

Materials: None

This is a simple way to introduce a topic. Some examples include jobs, cities, animals, etc. Have pairs of students write down A~Z on one piece of paper. Give them 2-4 minutes to think of one word/letter that fits that certain category. I make a rule that they can't use proper nouns. If you want to increase the difficulty or if you have a small class, you can make a rule that if two teams have the same word it doesn't count. This forces students to think more creatively.

Example: Topic = animals

A. Alligator

B. Bat

C. Cat

Etc.

Procedure:

1. In pairs, students write down the alphabet on a piece of paper.
2. Give students a topic and a certain amount of time.
3. Students think of one word per letter about the topic.
4. Check who has the most words at the end of the allotted time. Option for small classes: don't count repeated words so students have to think more creatively.

Boggle

Skills: Writing

Time: 10 minutes

Age: 8+

Materials: "Boggle" grid on PowerPoint, whiteboard or paper

You've probably played the word game Boggle before. You shake up the letters and then you have a certain amount of time to make some words with connecting letters. You can play it with your students but you don't need the actual Boggle game. Simply make up a grid on the whiteboard, PowerPoint or on a piece of paper. I make a 6x6 grid and put some obvious words in like the names of colors or animals, or the vocabulary that we've recently been studying. Then, students divide into pairs and have to make as many words as possible that are 4+ letters. You can give a bonus for longer words if you like. At the end, students count up how many points they have. You can double-check for any errors and then award a small prize to the winning team.

Procedure:

1. Prepare a "Boggle" grid.
2. Students divide into pairs and try to make as many words as possible with 4+ letters. Students cannot use the same letter in a single square twice within a single word.
3. Students add up points. The teacher checks the answers of the top two or three teams.

o	r	p	t	s	a
e	a	i	e	t	f
b	k	n	e	r	i
a	d	r	g	o	r
c	o	t	l	s	e
k	f	h	m	a	n

Some possible words from this board:

green, pink, rake, back, fire, fires, fast, road, rose

My World

Skills: Writing/Reading/Speaking/Listening

Time: 10-15 minutes

Age: 10+

Materials: None

This is an excellent icebreaker activity that you can do on the first day of class to introduce yourself and then have the students get to know one or two of their classmates. You start by drawing a big circle on the whiteboard with the title, "My World." Inside the circle there are various words, pictures or numbers that have some meaning to you. For example, inside my circle there might be 1979, blue, 37, a picture of two cats, and a mountain. The students would then have to make some guesses about why these things are special to me. The correct answers are: my birth year, favorite color, number of countries I've been to, my pets, and hiking which is my favorite hobby.

Procedure:
1. Draw a big circle on the board and write "My World" at the top. Put in some words, pictures or numbers inside the circle that have some meaning to you.
2. Have students guess what each thing means. Give hints if necessary.
3. Students prepare their own "world."
4. Students can play with a partner or in small groups of 3-4.

Odd One Out

Skills: Reading/Speaking or writing

Time: 5 minutes

Age: 7+

Materials: Groups of words

You can use Odd One Out to review vocabulary from the previous classes. Write up a few sets of vocabulary words on the whiteboard. I use four in one group, with one of them being the odd one out. For example: orange, cucumber, apple, banana. Cucumber is the odd one out because it's not a fruit.

Procedure:

1. Make 4-6 groups of four words, with one of them being unlike the others.
2. Put students in pairs and have them choose the odd word from each group and also write (or say) why they chose it. For example: Cucumber— not a fruit.

Part of Speech Review

Skills: Writing

Time: 5-10 minutes

Age: All

Materials: Worksheet/whiteboard/PowerPoint

Give the students several sentences and have them do one of the following: identify the part of speech of underlined words; circle (nouns/verbs/adjectives...); or add a word of the correct part of speech (fill in or multiple choice). Scaffold with an example of the activity done correctly as well as examples of the part of speech being focused on, such as a list of 5-6 nouns they know.

For an example of this activity, using possessive pronouns, check out: www.eslspeaking.org/part-of-speech.

Procedure:
1. In advance, prepare several sentences either on a worksheet or PowerPoint, or write them on the whiteboard.
2. Give students at least one example demonstrating how you would like the activity to be completed, for example, fill in the blank or circle the noun.
3. Begin the activity by eliciting from the students several examples of the given part of speech. Add to the list if necessary.
4. Give the students 2-5 minutes to complete the activity, depending on whether they need to write the sentences in their notebook or complete a worksheet.
5. Have students exchange papers and check answers.

Punctuation/Capitalization

Skills: Writing

Time: 5 minutes

Age: All

Materials: Worksheet/whiteboard/PowerPoint

Younger students and those whose first languages have different punctuation and/or capitalization rules than English need frequent practice in order to master correct usage. Have students correct several sentences, adding punctuation and capital letters as needed. For lower level and younger students, focus on one element at a time, such as the word "I" or using commas in a list. More advanced students can have a mix, but since this is a short activity, keep it to one correction per sentence. As with the Word Choice activity, students should write the sentences correctly. To make the activity easier, students can simply circle the correct word. To make the activity more challenging, have students fill in the blanks, with or without a word bank.

Procedure:
1. In advance, prepare several sentences either on a worksheet or PowerPoint, or write them on the whiteboard.
2. Give students at least one example demonstrating how you would like the activity to be completed, for example, add commas to a list.
3. Begin the activity by completing several examples of the activity as a class.
4. Give the students 2-5 minutes to complete the activity, depending on whether they need to write the sentences in their notebook or complete a worksheet.
5. Have students exchange papers and check answers.

Review Race

Skill: Writing

Time: 5 minutes

Age: 6+

Materials: Butcher or A3 paper (one piece per group) or whiteboard and markers (at least one marker per group)

Some students tend to look at each lesson as a discrete unit, forgetting that they are parts of a whole. This activity gets them using what they have learned. It's a great warm up activity. I've also used it before a test, both to boost their confidence and to give them one last bit of review time.

To play, divide students into groups of 4-5 and give each group at least one marker. If you are not using the whiteboard, also give each group one piece of A3 or butcher paper. Give students a time limit of 2-3 minutes to list all of the vocabulary words they can remember from the previous lesson. With higher-level classes, have students add a synonym, antonym, or brief definition. The group with the most correct words wins.

Procedure:

1. In advance, prepare markers, and optionally, a piece of A3 or butcher paper for each group.
2. Divide students into groups of 4-5.
3. Have students work together to list all of the vocabulary they can remember from the previous lesson within the time limit of 2-3 minutes.
4. For higher-level classes, have students add a synonym, antonym or brief

definition of each word.

5. The group with the most correct words wins.

Sentence Word Order

Skills: Writing

Time: 5-10 minutes

Age: All

Materials: Sentence cards, worksheet/whiteboard/PowerPoint

     Students whose first languages have different subject/verb/object order than English need practice with the correct grammatical structures. Give students several sentences with some words in the wrong order. Have students rewrite the sentences correctly. Here's an example of the sentence word order activity: www.eslspeaking.org/sentence-word-order.

Sentence card version: you will need to have one card with several sentences or several cards with one sentence each per student/pair/small group. This version is better for having students work together, adding a speaking component to the activity, or as an early finisher activity.

Worksheet version: Give students space to correctly write the sentences or choose the correct of two options.

Whiteboard/PowerPoint version: Give students several sentences for them to write correctly in their notebooks.

Teaching Tip:

Sentence cards are simply cards with sentences. This creates a bit of a wild card element, since everyone gets something different, and is good for classes with students who tend to copy one another or for using as an early finisher activity. Don't forget to laminate them and begin with an example.

Procedure:

1. Prepare several sentences either on sentence cards, a worksheet or PowerPoint, or write them on the whiteboard.
2. Give students at least one example demonstrating how you would like the activity to be completed, showing a mixed up sentence with the correction.
3. Begin the activity by completing several examples of the activity as a class.
4. Give the students 2-5 minutes to complete the activity, depending on whether they need to write the sentences in their notebook or complete a worksheet.
5. Have students exchange papers and check answers.

Subject-Predicate Practice

Skills: Writing

Time: 5-10 minutes

Age: All

Materials: Worksheet/whiteboard/PowerPoint

This is a quick grammar practice activity. Depending on the level of the class, have them simply identify subjects and predicates, complete sentences by adding one or the other, or have students add details to the subject or predicate (adjective/adverb practice).

Procedure:

1. In advance, prepare several sentences on a worksheet or PowerPoint or write them on the whiteboard.
2. Give students at least one example demonstrating how you would like the activity to be completed, for example, circle the subject or complete the sentence by adding a subject.
3. Begin the activity by completing several examples of the activity as a class.
4. Give the students 3-5 minutes to complete the activity, depending on whether they need to write the sentences in their notebook or complete a worksheet.
5. Have students exchange papers and check answers. If they are creating their own subjects or predicates, you may want to collect the papers to check yourself.

Word Choice

Skills: Writing
Time: 5-10 minutes
Age: All
Materials: Worksheet/whiteboard/PowerPoint

This can be used to review subject/object pronouns, adjectives/adverbs, etc. by having students choose the correct word. Give the students several sentences with a blank and two possible answers. Students should write the sentences correctly. To make the activity easier, students can simply circle the correct word. To make the activity more challenging, have students fill in the blanks, with or without a word bank.

Procedure:
1. In advance, prepare several sentences either on a worksheet or PowerPoint, or write them on the whiteboard.
2. Give students at least one example demonstrating how you would like the activity to be completed, for example, fill in the blank with the adjective.
3. Begin the activity by eliciting from the students several examples of the two options they have, such as subject and object pronouns, and when to use them. Add to the list, if necessary.
4. Give the students 2-5 minutes to complete the activity, depending on whether they need to write the sentences in their notebook or complete a worksheet.
5. Have students exchange papers and check answers.

Words in Words

Skills: Writing

Time: 5-10 minutes

Age: 8+

Materials: Worksheet/whiteboard or PowerPoint

You probably did this when you were in school. Give students a word and have them make as many words as possible using the letters in that word. For example: "vacation" = a, on, no, act, action, taco, ant, van. You can give a point for each word, so that the student with the most words wins, or give more points for longer words. When time is up (about five minutes), show students the possible answers.

Wordles.com has a tool that allows you to type in a word and get the possible words. For vacation, they listed 45 words, some of which I should have thought of myself and some of which are "Scrabble words." Since your students will not possibly know all of these words, it is up to you whether you show all the answers or an abridged list.

Procedure:

1. In advance, prepare a long word and write it on the whiteboard or a PowerPoint or give students individual worksheets.
2. Give students a time limit of about five minutes to make words from the letters in the word.
3. To make it a competition, when time is up, you can give students points for each word.
4. When the activity is finished, show students all of the possible words they could have made. You can get these from www.wordles.com.

Before You Go

Before you go, please leave a review wherever you got this book. I appreciate your feedback and it will help other teachers like yourself find this book. My goal is to spread some ESL teaching awesome to the world!

Jackie Bolen around the Internet

ESL Speaking (www.eslspeaking.org)

YouTube (https://www.youtube.com/c/jackiebolen)

Instagram (www.instagram.com/jackie.bolen)

Pinterest (www.pinterest.com/eslspeaking)

Made in the USA
Monee, IL
15 October 2024